PERFORMANCE COMPENSATION FOR STAKEHOLDERS™

PERFORMANCE COMPENSATION FOR STAKEHOLDERS™

14 Prerequisites for Success

Michael T. Higgins and Michael M. Higgins

DJI Publishing
LINCOLN, NEBRASKA

First printing 2002

ISBN 0-9711808-4-9

LCCN 2001132984

ATTENTION CORPORATIONS, UNIVERSITIES, COLLEGES, AND PROFESSIONAL ORGANIZATIONS: Quantity discounts are available on bulk purchases of this book for educational, gift purposes, or as premiums for increasing magazine subscriptions or renewals. Special books or book excerpts can also be created to fit specific needs. For information, please contact DJI Publishing, 1919 South 40th Street, Suite 213, Lincoln, NE 68506; ph. 402-489-0300.

TABLE OF CONTENTS

PART 1—The Need for a New Approach to Compensation

PART II—Performance Compensation for Stakeholders Methodology

PART III—*STAKEHOLDERS*: A Catalyst for Positive Change

APPENDICES

This book defines a management and leadership system that I believe is a prerequisite for any company that wishes to maximize its performance. The underlying performance compensation methodology is based on five very important observations.

1. I have never met anyone who could get excited about making money for someone else.

2. All organizations, all business units, teams and departments, no matter how large or small, no matter how successful, have limited resources. How management invests those limited resources will determine whether or not the organization will survive. It will determine whether or not it will prosper, and, even more important, whether or not it will realize it's full potential.

3. The business world is in the midst of significant transformation. Peter Drucker[1] has even proposed that, "Traditional capitalism is evolving into a 'post-capitalistic' society which blurs the definitions of owners, managers and workers beyond the changes that we have already experienced." This new paradigm creates "knowledge workers" who, when appropriately applying their knowledge to work, can significantly improve productivity.

4. We have, indeed, experienced the dramatic transition from an industrial society to an information society, and yet nothing significant has changed in the way we compensate people beyond base salary.

5. I have always been frustrated with the way I was compensated and the way we compensated the people I worked with. Now, after studying traditional performance compensation techniques for the past 18 years, I am convinced that there never has been a successful management team or workforce that actually did what they were paid to do.

"STAKEHOLDERS" is a methodology that I created in 1983 and tested for more than five years in eight companies before introducing it to the business world as a proven system. It begins with the premise that base salaries should be managed toward midpoint in the marketplace and that all compensation beyond base salary should be tied to performance. My goal was to take a completely fresh approach by designing a performance compensation system from the ground up as if there were no traditional methods of rewarding people for performance.

The methodology, then, provides for a system of performance management that incorporates 14 significant departures from traditional methodology. It creates an environment where everyone thinks and works like an owner because management recognizes the significant untapped potential of its "knowledge workers."

In recent years my son, Michael M. Higgins, has contributed significantly to refining and broadening *"STAKEHOLDERS."* He has converted the methodology into a very contemporary, state-of-the-art information technology system. This new infrastructure has enabled its transformation into a comprehensive performance management and leadership system from which a management team can align performance compensation to the strategic planning and budgeting processes.

—Michael T. Higgins

PART 1

The Need for a New Approach to Reward Compensation

CHAPTER 1

Traditional Compensation Methods: No Longer Valid, No Longer Relevant

"Some people look reality right in the eye and deny it."
—AUTHOR UNKNOWN

Since the 1960s, we have been involved in a dramatic transition from a national industrial economy driven by manual labor to a global, high-tech and service economy driven by information. Yet very little has changed in our basic thinking about compensation. Rooted in the Industrial Revolution, traditional compensation methodologies in use today are an accumulation of responses to the concern of the moment. This hodgepodge of traditional methodologies is increasingly invalid and inadequate for the 21st century. One symptom of this mismatch is that traditional reward programs reinforce entitlements. Another is the creation of adversaries among ownership, management and the workforce. Rather, contemporary compensation programs must create a partnership among all stakeholders.

Another symptom of the mismatch between traditional compensation methods and today's needs is the widely discussed concern about inequity of compensation—"income inequality." However, all too often the focus is on the amount of executive compensation and always on, "How much?" More fundamentally,

3

whether it is executive or anyone's base compensation, subjective merit adjustments, performance rewards, or retirement contributions, we should not be asking, "How much?" Rather, we should be asking, "What for?" This is because compensation inequities only arise when reward compensation is not tied to results and the creation of long-term shareholder value.

The Contradictions

I have always been frustrated with the way I have been compensated and the way I have previously compensated people who have worked with me.

Before I became a management consultant, I was asked to become president of a bank that had nearly failed. During my initial interview, the board of directors and the majority stockholders agreed with my plan on what we had to do to create a banking company that would become competitive. We recognized that the four most important influences on being competitive had been ignored for nearly three years as the previous management team worked out their loan problems. Investment in people, facilities, product development or information systems all had been short-changed because the team did not have the time or capital to invest in those four critical influences.

Therefore, we agreed that we had to recruit good people, as well as invest in training the remaining staff to become more proficient. We agreed to invest in product development and management information systems. We agreed that all of our facilities, our main office and satellite offices, had to be renovated to attract consumers to do business with us. We agreed to invest in people, facilities, product development and systems.

Then they (the board of directors) *proposed to pay me not to do it*. My compensation included a generous base salary and an even more generous bonus. However, the bonus was based on maximizing annual profit—the bigger the annual profit, the bigger the bonus.

As with more than 90% of CEOs and management teams in the United States, I was hired to make a company successful and remain competitive, but rewarded not to do it. When executives are rewarded to maximize annual profitability, they are being rewarded *not* to invest in people, facilities, product development and systems. They are being rewarded to maximize short-term, annual earnings at the expense of long-term earnings, long-term shareholder value and long-term viability of their company.

Again and again, our management team would discuss, "Should we do what we are paid to do or what we were hired to do?" "Should we try to maximize our bonus by maximizing short-term annual profit or should we invest in the future by committing to the game plan that we had all agreed upon in order to rebuild the business?"

Obviously, like most successful executive management teams, *we did not do what we were paid to do*. We committed to invest in the future at the expense of maximizing our annual bonus because the basis for our reward was diametrically opposed to what the board and the shareholders wanted us to do.

It was not the first time I had encountered the contradictions of traditional compensation. Early in my career, I was in industrial sales with the Aluminum Company of America. One day it occurred to me that I was spending as much time with order taking, the sales administrative group, shipping coordinators and quality control people in our manufacturing plants as I was with my customers. Later on, when I became regional sales manager for eleven states, I continued to spend much of my time with the support people throughout the company. Now I was spending time not only with the administrative group, shipping and quality control, but also with human resources, accounting, and MIS. I spent an enormous amount of time with these support staffs because they were the people who made the sales force successful. We could not be successful without them. We could do poorly in sales—that is, we could fail by ourselves. We could not be successful, however, without total commitment from everyone who supported the sales effort. Therefore, it became very apparent to me early in my career that there were two equally important business units on every sales team—the promise makers and the promise keepers.

There was no denying that each of these departments supported the success of the sales team, from retaining business by creating quality products to providing accurate reporting for all of management and the customers. Once the sales team opened the door, it was the support groups behind the scenes that ultimately closed the deal and kept the business. Had any of the support areas performed poorly, our business would have declined dramatically.

Yet, only the sales team and senior management team received a significant bonus for performance. Despite their clear contribution to the performance of the organization, those among the support staff did not participate in any reward program related to performance. They may have received profit-sharing or a Christmas bonus, but these had nothing to do with how they actually contributed to the overall performance of the company.

Unfortunately, this is typical for support teams. Too many people perceive that support teams have no real effect upon an organization's performance since they do not have a direct role in closing business. Even support people perceive their responsibilities as a matter of function rather than results. The misperception is that their function can be carried out by anyone with the appropriate training.

Nothing could be further from reality. Support teams enable the rest of the organization to perform to the best of its ability. They empower others, and provide swift and immediate service, all of which directly impacts existing customers and is a deciding factor in whether or not an organization gets and retains new customers.

Once I was speaking at a national convention in Boston. After I completed my prepared talk, I asked if there were any questions. One CEO stood up and stated, "Mike, what you say sounds good, and feels good, but, if you were really honest, you would admit that there are only two or three people in any organization who really make a difference!" I asked him if he really believed that and how many employees were in his company. His answer was that he did believe that and his company had 458 employees. I then asked: "If 455 people don't make a difference in your company's performance, why don't you send them all home for the next ninety days and then re-evaluate what sort of impact they have upon sales, customer retention and corporate-wide performance?"

The Alternative Approach

My experiences led me to design a compensation program that was in the best interest of everyone in an organization. This became a unique methodology we now call *Performance Compensation for Stakeholders*—"*STAKEHOLDERS*," for short. It is significantly different from traditional compensation programs. First, as suggested by the term stakeholders, every employee has a significant stake in the company's performance. Therefore, it ties all employees into a reward pool distributed according to each team and individual's contribution toward achieving the organization's success. Second, performance criteria rest on an organizational strategy to achieve not just short-term profitability, but long-term shareholder value and, therefore, long-term viability of the company. Third, the achievement of long-term viability can only be realized when everyone understands the implications of competitive advantage created by exceptional customer service.

Maximizing Long-Term Shareholder Value

We have subtitled this book "*How to Maximize Long-Term Stakeholder Value*" to underline the dichotomy between organizational priorities and traditional compensation methods. My experience as a CEO provided a glimpse of the dilemma that compensating for maximizing annual profitability poses for executives who are actually chartered to achieve long-term competitiveness for their organization. We can further see the need for a new approach to compensation by examining the consequences in terms of organizational strategy.

An organization can effectively pursue only one of four master strategies: maximize profit, maximize growth, balance profit with growth, or position the company to merge or sell. (See Figure 1-1, next page.)

Each strategy will have its own priorities and action plans. A strategy to maximize profit is a survival strategy where a company is failing and has to create capital to cover payroll and other operating expenses. If an organization's master strategy is to maximize profit, its action plans will include tactics to raise prices at the expense of market share. It will sell off fixed assets. It will not

7

Figure 1-1 Balance of Profit, Growth, Quality, and Productivity

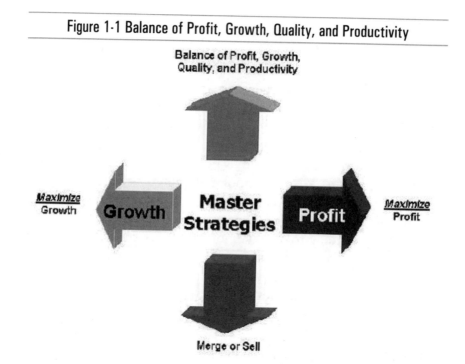

invest in people and training. It will de-emphasize investments in systems, product development, facilities or expertise that look toward its future ability to meet market requirements for quality goods and services.

The master strategy that is the opposite of maximizing profit is to maximize growth. Here, the priority is to gain more customers or market share. It requires action plans to lower prices and/or to invest in new facilities, product development, product acquisition, additional skills, expertise, and systems—all at the expense of profitability.

It can be seen that both the maximizing profit and maximizing growth strategies are short-term strategies. An organization cannot follow a strategy to maximize profit for too long without driving all of its customers away. A growth-maximizing strategy is also very short term. It cannot be orchestrated for the long term because an organization using it will likely acquire a lot of new customers, but it will not create or maintain enough earnings to continue serving the expanded client base.

We can also see that many of the most widely used traditional approaches to compensation are also an operational contradiction. The vast majority of management bonuses, profit-sharing programs and pension plans are designed around the short-term master strategy to maximize annual profit. At the same time, the sales force and sometimes other customer contact people are rewarded for short-term sales, sales referral or other growth goals. Rarely are sales or volume goals coordinated with reward systems that focus on *profitable* sales or *profitable* volume.

The master strategy to merge or sell the organization is typically the shortest term of all. We call it an opportunistic strategy; for example, some group offers ten times the book value of the company and at that moment the company has a new master strategy—to merge or sell.

Finally, the only master strategy that will maximize long-term shareholder value and therefore the long-term viability of any organization is the strategy to balance profit with growth, and at the same time balance these with the corollary quality and productivity elements of long-term success. (See Figure 1-2.)

Figure 1-2 Balance of Profit, Growth, Quality, and Productivity

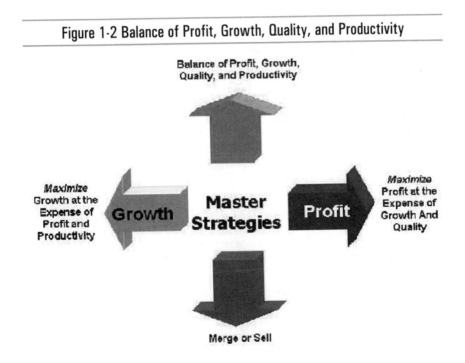

"STAKEHOLDERS" provides the framework to balance profit with growth, quality and productivity. The methodology encompasses all levels of an organization in a reward program that is reconciled with the organization's master strategy. In turn, it assures the continuing viability of the organization and continuous service to its constituency.

Stakeholders

Who are the stakeholders? The term stakeholders has entered the business vocabulary in a broad sense to signify that everyone connected to an organization is a stakeholder in its well-being. Quite rightly this includes shareholders, a board of directors, management, the entire workforce and even an organization's customers or clients.

In practice, the *"STAKEHOLDERS"* concept centers on the workforce because their contribution to an organization's success is too often unrecognized, and that contribution is least understood by the workforce itself. All too often the vast majority of the workforce thinks in terms of what they do, rather than what they accomplish.

Secondly, the workforce does not perceive their vested interest in their company. However, in most for-profit organizations (with the exception of closely held companies), each employee has a greater vested interest in their company than any one shareholder. Each employees' vested interest includes their experience, their expertise and the very financial security of their families. Shareholders in widely held companies do not have a critical amount of their net worth invested in any one company. Most employees do.

The other members of the *"STAKEHOLDERS"* concept, the shareholders, board and clients, also participate and benefit because the concept allows the company to maximize its profitability potential as well as maximize its service and product quality.

"STAKEHOLDERS" is a methodology. Therefore, its successful implementation involves considerable re-thinking. Employees must be taught to understand the implications of their vested interest. It takes a total understanding of those implications to

motivate themselves to think in terms of maximizing their contribution because that is how they will earn significant rewards for their work. That is also how they reinforce long-term job security. Equally important, management has to drop the traditional mindset that harks back to an era of manual labor and paternal ownership that is no longer relevant.

Traditional perspectives evolve around the belief that top-level management and ownership made the decisions and were responsible for the activity that led to improved organization performance and impact on the bottom line. Those perspectives were perhaps arrived at logically in that managers at that point in time often did have the most experience, better or more formal education, and a track record that spoke of their aptitude as managers. Unfortunately, that mindset has persisted as the backdrop for today's traditional compensation programs, and it is no longer relevant.

Contributions to traditional pension and profit-sharing plans and annual bonuses are most frequently arbitrary, created in a paternal fashion after results have been achieved. These rewards are not based on any predetermined level of achievement and thus leave the employee unaware of any particular attributes that warrant the bonus other than "doing a good job." Therefore, this type of reward too often comes to be expected as an entitlement because the participants do not relate the reward to their contribution to the company's performance. Equally detrimental, traditional reward programs never teach the participants what they can do to improve their performance and their contribution to the company.

Perceived compensation inequities when management is rewarded without substantiated performance also contribute to the demise of morale in all organizations. These apparent inequities have grown the rift between management and other employees, and often impose a proverbial wagon-circling mentality because of the segregation of the basis for management's reward from that of all others in the organization.

Traditional reward programs also promote internal competition at the expense of corporate-wide cooperation. An organization thinks it has implemented an enticing new incentive reward that will stimulate growth but instead ignites distracting conflict among individuals vying to claim credit for capturing the new business, for having first seen the new account, first heard of the new business opportunity, first contacted the new client.

Most importantly, traditional methods fail to tap the inherent entrepreneurial instincts of all employees. By leaving out large parts of the workforce from a reward that meaningfully ties their efforts to clear organizational objectives, we have grown cultures in which function is the only context for their work. We communicate that theirs is a position to which organizational goals do not relate, that their function is to support others in pursuit of such goals, but that they themselves have no effect upon the bottom line.

Most of the time, employees strive to do their jobs well. They do things right. As many studies have shown, however, they often are not doing the right things because they lack understanding of their organization's priorities and how their work contributes to achievement of those priorities. A reward program can only become relevant when the corporate culture shifts to creating a sense of ownership among all employees throughout the organization. Then, from a functional focus on doing things right, they can focus on doing the right things to promote the organization's goals and satisfy their own interests as stakeholders.

Implementing the New Approach

"STAKEHOLDERS" enables the pursuit of long-term goals that are the true ideal of most organizations. The intent must be to distribute a reward pool based on predetermined levels of performance. Results are a case of the proverbial rising tide that lifts all ships.

The methodology has now been successfully adopted by nearly 500 organizations in the U.S., western Europe and the Pacific Rim. Successful "STAKEHOLDERS" organizations have experienced annual bonuses of 50% of their current base salaries for their contribution to doubling, tripling and even quadrupling overall net income for their respective companies.

Summary

Rooted in the industrial revolution, 20th-century compensation programs have fallen short of purpose on numerous fronts. They hone in upon a singular short-term master strategy and ignore long-term corporate objectives. They are arbitrarily and subjectively devised to promote antithetical focus and strategy between lower-level and upper-level management. They foster internal competition, lead to perceptions of unfairness, and omit large numbers of employees from the opportunity to participate in reward for achievement. The result is apathy and cynicism that is often directed at perceived inequities in compensation between management and other employees.

Performance Compensation for Stakeholders™ (*"STAKE-HOLDERS"*) is an alternative and proven approach quite different from traditional methodologies. The first four companies who installed it in 1989 still use it as their basis for variable pay.

The intended goals of all compensation programs should include maximizing long-term shareholder value, long-term viability of the company, and, thereby, long-term job security. An organization will accomplish this only by balancing growth with profit, quality and productivity priorities. Programs with strategies that do not include all of these critical influences will inevitably fall into alignment with short-term priorities and short-term thinking at the expense of long-term corporate performance.

Fortunately, some companies have realized the value of the contribution of each person in their organization. Few, however, link their reward programs to the overall corporate strategy, and none of them reconcile the reward payout to the financial results created by the four prerequisite influences.

A reward program will become relevant when the corporate culture creates a sense of ownership in all employees throughout the organization. Everyone must understand the corporate objectives and priorities. Everyone must understand how their work contributes to the performance of their team, which affects department or division performance, which ultimately supports the total organization's performance. Concentration on individual activity or *function* must be replaced with concentration on individual *performance*, and the traditional focus upon doing things right must be replaced with focus upon doing the right things, right.

The restructuring of goal achievement begins with a commitment to educate everyone within the organization on how they can contribute to the achievement of those goals. We must replace traditional paradigms with realistic strategies that exploit the talent and skills of our greatest resource, our people. We must employ their innate ability to perform, gain recognition for performance, contribute, work as part of a successful team, and grow. These are qualities all of our people possess but until now have been forced to deny.

Long-term viability of the organization, long-term shareholder value, and long-term job security will be achieved only after tearing down traditional management reward systems. They will only be achieved after destroying the perception of reward segregation, incorporating the talents and strengths of every employee, and guiding them toward the unlimited and untapped potential that exists within all organizations.

Everyone will acknowledge that our economy has completed its transition from a labor-driven industrial society to one driven by information. It is time to replace the traditional compensation systems with systems relevant to the new environment.

CHAPTER 2

A Strategy for Change: Performance Compensation for Stakeholders

*"If you do not look at things on a
large scale first, it will be difficult for you
to master any strategy."*
—MIYAMOTO MUSASHI (1643)

Suppose you were to gather 100 executives in a room and asked them to design a performance compensation program, from the ground up, as if there were no traditional method of rewarding people. How would they create an equitable and meaningful program?

Would they reward people for the achievement of short-term priorities or on long-term priorities that would ensure long-term viability of the organization and long-term shareholder value?

Would they reward people for things they do or for what they accomplish, i.e., would they reward for activity or for results?

Would they cap performance rewards or take all caps off and allow everyone to share in windfalls as well as shortfalls, just like shareholders?

Would they wait until year-end to determine "how the company did" to create reward or would they build performance reward into corporate strategy and planning?

Would they reward arbitrarily, or would they reward people for performance based on mathematically calculated, i.e., precise, added value that they contribute to the organization?

Would they have many different incentive programs going without reconciliation with the overall performance of the organization, or would they want a reward system that tied department, division, team, satellite office and individual performance into total organization performance?

Would they create a reward system that has nothing to do with an organization's vision and mission or a reward system that teaches everyone to understand where the organization is going, how to get there and how each employee contributes?

Would they want a compensation program in which very few employees knew the value of the total organization's compensation package, or would they want to teach everyone in the organization about the value of all compensation, benefits and reward?

Would they view compensation as a human resource department function or as the key management tool to focus everyone in the organization on maximizing performance?

These are among the contrasts that point up significant differences between traditional reward compensation programs and the new approach we call *Performance Compensation for Stakeholders*™ (*"STAKEHOLDERS"*). Some traditional performance programs have some of the positive elements (Figure 2-1); however, the *"STAKEHOLDERS"* approach is driven by all of these elements working together.

The unique aspects of *"STAKEHOLDERS"* fly in the face of traditional methods. They require re-thinking of old practices on the part of both employees and management. Additionally, methods in use today rarely include everyone. Never is performance weighted and penalized for under-achievement. Typically, an organization has a whole range of incentive and reward programs going on and the value of the total reward is never reconciled with the actual value of achievement.

Figure 2-1: Performance Compensation Comparison

	Traditional	*"STAKEHOLDERS"*
1. Focus:	Short-Term Results	Strategic Priorities
2. Participation:	Limited to "Key" Personnel	Everyone
3. Funding:	Discretionary	100% Self-Funding
4. Base Pay:	Sometimes At Risk	Never At Risk
5. Education:	Minimal/Lacking	Creates "Business Literacy"
6. Creates:	Super Stars and Adversaries	Super Teams, Partnerships
7. Reward For:	Activity	Results
8. Reward For:	Profit **or** Growth **or** Quality **or** Productivity	Profit **and** Growth **and** Quality **and** Productivity "Balanced Scorecard"
9. Reward:	After the Fact, Subjective	Predetermined
10. Weighting of Measures:	None or Subjective	Mathematically Computed
11. Cap on Reward:	Cap on Bonus	Unlimited Reward Opportunity
12. Underachievement:	No Consequence	Penalizes Reward Pool
13. Reconciliation:	Reward Does Not Reconcile With Overall Corporate Performance	Reward Reconciles with Performance
14. Ownership	None	Allows Everyone to Think and Work Like an Owner

Participation

Traditional performance management and performance reward programs focus on management, managers and supervisors, and sales and/or customer contract personnel.

17

Rather, performance compensation must recognize that everyone in the organization makes a significant contribution to the total results. Therefore, we must reward everyone for their contribution to their organization's level of achievement, as well as for their contribution to division, department, team and/or satellite office achievement. Reward must not be exclusionary. Secondly, everyone must be involved in performance reward if an organization is ever to realize its full potential.

Yet, many who consider themselves specialists in compensation programs recommend that significant reward programs be limited to management only, or limit it to managers and customer contact people.

Creating recognition and reward programs for *only* management and customer contact people is very shortsighted. In an economic environment that increasingly depends on service and support, limiting significant reward to management and customer contact people demonstrates to the whole organization that the all-important support staff is not important!

To the many executives and compensation specialists who argue this position, I say, "If you *don't* think your support staff is just as important as managers and customer contact people, send them home. You're wasting a lot of overhead you do not believe in."

The absurdity of this mindset is illustrated by a hypothetical scene that I often share with boards of directors and management teams. Imagine your favorite professional football team's locker room as they prepare for the Super Bowl playoffs. The coach gathers the team before going out on the field and says:

> *"Gentlemen, today we begin the playoffs toward our ultimate goal—winning the Super Bowl. You all know our game plan. You all know your responsibilities. And you all know that our ultimate achievement is totally dependent upon each and every player playing at his optimum potential. Before we begin, I want you all to know that if we do win the Super Bowl, the entire bonus package will be equally divided among our quarterback, the owners, and me. Now let's get out there and win!"*

18

Well, you can imagine what would happen. The quarterback would spend the entire game on his back. And there would be no second playoff game, much less a Super Bowl appearance.

Unfortunately, that's exactly what American industry has been doing to their team for at least the last 40 years. Many managers think that their "incentive pool" will be diluted if the opportunity for reward is afforded to everyone. The fact is that when a properly designed reward program includes everyone, management benefits more because of the increased performance from the entire organization.

Maximizing long-term shareholder value to ensure the long-term viability of a company requires an understanding of and a commitment to strategic priorities throughout the entire organization. Including everyone in reward opportunities means that everyone in the organization deserves to understand how the company keeps score and how the company wins. If they do not even understand how the company scores, how in the world can they ever think about how to maximize their potential?

The Importance of Reconciliation

Some companies are beginning to realize the need to recognize and reward everyone's performance. Yet few companies link the various reward programs to overall strategy and none reconcile reward and levels of accomplishment to the organization's financial results.

Pension and profit-sharing plans and annual bonuses are often arbitrary, created after results have been achieved, and established by boards of directors in a paternal activity. The result is that employees are not aware why they have been compensated and they think in terms of these programs as additional wages. The reward is not based on predetermined levels of achievement. Therefore, during the performance period, employees do not tie their work to the organization's performance. After-the-fact arbitrary rewards are good savings programs, but they have nothing to do with creating a motivational environment to improve, much less maximize, performance.

19

Arbitrary reward also leaves a bad taste in everyone's mouth. The employees do not know why they are being rewarded so they don't know if they received too much or too little. And the frustration of the board of directors and management is the same. Because reward is not tied to precise levels of performance, nobody knows whether the allocation, often very costly, is too much or too little for the level of achievement.

ESOPs (employee stock-ownership plans) are one of today's reward systems that pretend to equate to the implications of ownership. Yet they provide no direction or information on how each and every employee can contribute to company results. Therefore, the ESOP as a stand alone reward instrument has no significant relevance to maximizing performance.

Tying Reward to Company Strategy

A relevant reward program will create a sense of ownership throughout the organization because everyone understands where the organization is going and each and every employee understands how they contribute to that journey. Each *"STAKEHOLDERS"* employee must also learn how their team, department, and division's contribution supports the total corporate result. That level of business literacy is prerequisite for the organization to maximize its potential.

In Chapter 1, we discussed the importance of the master strategy and prioritizing a balance of profit and growth with quality and productivity. This strategy will result in providing long-term shareholder value and long-term job security with significant compensation opportunities, i.e., long-term stakeholder value.

Therefore, the *"STAKEHOLDERS"* approach is based on multiple goal achievement, that is, a predetermined balance of the four elements: profit, growth, quality and productivity. Secondly, in order to preclude arbitrary reward values, each of the four influences must be mathematically weighted to ensure that all reward is explicitly tied to the value of improved performance.

The importance of multiple goal achievement, i.e., rewarding for all four influences, is illustrated by what happens when rewards are created for only one influence on achievement. If you reward for profit only, people will focus on profit at the expense of growth, quality and productivity. Similarly, if you reward for volume or growth only, people will concentrate on volume at the expense of profit, quality and productivity. As long as rewards are limited to fewer than all four critical influences, employees will always concentrate on what they are being rewarded for because management is rewarding them to ignore the other influences.

"*STAKEHOLDERS*" includes a methodology for linking performance with corporate goals and reconciling performance with annual results. The methodology is based on Key Performance Indicators (KPIs).

How KPIs are used is critical. While some methodologies incorporate various KPIs, they rarely combine and balance profit, growth, quality and productivity. And, typically, they are arbitrarily weighted by management and/or the board of directors. In contrast, the "*STAKEHOLDERS*" methodology mathematically calculates the value of increased performance within each KPI as it relates to total improved performance throughout the organization.

That step is prerequisite to linking reward precisely to predetermined levels of increased performance. Only with precise calculations can managers and directors establish a minimum baseline of performance to justify base salaries and overhead and then confidently create a sharing of the increased performance based on the value of the increased performance beyond baseline.

Uniquely, the approach *never* caps the amount of reward a participant can earn, and it penalizes for failure to meet baseline, or minimum levels of performance tied to balancing profit and growth with quality and productivity.

Most reward programs have a cap on the amount of reward a participant can earn. That is because traditional approaches think in terms of windfalls and "unearned" improved performance. Contemporary thinkers are aware that caps on reward put a cap on performance. Employees will commit to work smarter to improve long-term performance if they participate in an organization's windfalls as well as its shortfalls, just like the shareholders.

Similarly, other compensation programs reward people for achieving various levels of performance, but rarely, if ever, include

21

a consequence for not achieving minimal levels of performance. This lack of penalty is the single most important reason individuals do not motivate themselves to achieve high performance.

Results Versus Activity

Measuring performance for results rather than activity is another unique objective of the *"STAKEHOLDERS"* methodology.

Too often, reward programs reward for activity rather than results. In *"STAKEHOLDERS,"* activity is to be measured and managed; only results are rewarded. The greatest downside for rewarding people for activity rather than results is that reward is never reconciled with the actual profit performance the organization achieves.

For example, training programs are very important activities prerequisite to successful performance. However, reward should not be based on how many people attended how many hours of training or how many hours of training are provided. Performance reward should be based on the results of training measured by improvement in the organization's overall performance or on the results of training measured by division, department, team or individual performance.

The key is to manage training and educate trainees and trainers about what they must do to achieve performance, i.e., results. Keeping score is essential, but people are far more likely to get excited about measuring results connected to compensation than about rewarding activity.

Measuring for results stimulates people to think about individual priorities and the mission that each and every individual deserves to create for themselves so that they concentrate on what it is that they want to contribute and then prioritize what they should do.

For example, parking valets too often think their job responsibility is to park and retrieve cars. That is not something to get very excited about. Rather, they should perceive their jobs as one of helping people with convenience and comfort. People get excited about helping people.

Too many bankers think in terms of making loans. Rather, their mission should be to help clients maximize their financial potential.

A secretary's position is normally perceived in terms of creating correspondence and messages. Rather, their mission should be perceived as assisting an organization's clients to better understand how the company can help them achieve their goals or improve their quality of life.

In manufacturing, it is not the number of widgets that go through a machine that is most important. Rather, we should be reinforcing a mindset that focuses on creating a quality product to improve quality of life for customers who use it or on improving the financial potential of the companies who buy the products.

People want more than anything else to have pride in their work. In order to have that kind of pride, they must understand how they contribute to results.

Implementing "STAKEHOLDERS" entails both a technical process and an educational process.

Summary

This chapter has described some of the important ways in which "STAKEHOLDERS" contrasts sharply with traditional compensation methodologies. Many companies, depending on their size, have many different incentive reward programs but these are never reconciled with the actual results of the organization. Nor are the reward programs coordinated with one another.

"STAKEHOLDERS" requires that all reward programs reconcile within each department and division and with the overall achievement of the organization. This unique feature ensures that all performance reward is within the scope of the long-term priorities of the organization—the balance of profit, growth, quality and productivity.

It also ensures that the opportunity to share in performance reward is available to everyone in the organization, is based on precise measurement rather than arbitrarily bestowed, and encourages performance for results, not activity.

Through these characteristics and as the name clearly states, *Performance Compensation for Stakeholders*™ creates a sense of ownership throughout an organization. Everyone understands where the organization is going and each and every employee understands how his or her contribution relates to that journey and the organization's success.

CHAPTER 3

Success by Maximizing Human Potential

*"It's not the critic who counts....
The credit belongs to the man who strives
valiantly...who at the best knows in the end
the triumph of high achievement; and who
at the worst, if he fails, at least fails while
daring greatly; so that his place shall never
be with those cold timid souls who know
neither victory or defeat."*
—THEODORE ROOSEVELT

What is success? Success has been defined as the progressive realization of goals that are worthwhile to the individual and to other people. Therefore, people without goals are by definition incapable of being successful.

People with goals have purpose. Purpose provides freedom from ambiguity, freedom from irrelevant distractions, and freedom from insecurity.

Goals begin with vision. Successful leaders will formulate their professional vision to *create a work environment where stakeholders are as excited about coming to work as they are about going home to their families.* That has nothing to do with re-establishing work priorities in place of family. Rather, it recognizes the fact that most people spend a greater portion of their waking hours at work. Work environments should be as satisfying as non-working environments.

When people feel enthusiastic about their work environment, they will create an enthusiastic belief in their company or institution, which is essential to their maximizing their contribution to that organization.

Setting New Goals

Success for stakeholders depends on their achieving levels of performance beyond current levels and/or levels of performance beyond a minimum standard of expectation. The overall goal is to maximize the potential of everyone involved.

One of the first two organizations to adopt the *"STAKEHOLD-ERS"* methodology was a high-performing bank in the northeastern suburbs of Los Angeles. Another was a very low-performing bank in rural Indiana. The high-performing bank had realized a level of high performance, but they had difficulty in taking their organization to the next level of performance.

When they incorporated *"STAKEHOLDERS,"* they literally doubled their level of profitability during the next four years (Figure 3-1) and became the 20th most consistently profitable bank in the United States for the previous five years.

Figure 3-1 Earnings Per Share (EPS)

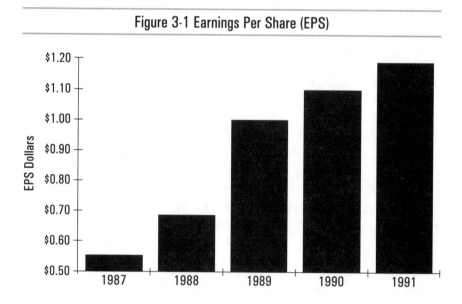

Concurrently, the relatively low-performing bank, which had earned less than 3% on equity during the previous decade, realized 20.2% return on equity and became a top-ten-performing bank in the very first year they applied the methodology.

In each case, the methodology created a working environment in which everyone became so enthusiastic about their company because they learned to approach their work as if they were owners. For example, the low-performing bank in its very first year generated an average of 23 referrals from each of its employees. It closed 57.3% of all referrals and that alone tripled the bank's pretax income from the previous year.

Similarly, a vertical wholesale-retail lumber business began to realize its full potential early on. For example, the dispatch manager reported that a day does not go by that he does not hear at least one truck driver directing the people on the loading dock to "get that load on correctly and don't damage it, because you know that impacts our margin." The manager related that he "never thought that he would ever hear that type of conversation, not in a lifetime." Today he hears it every day because focused people think like owners.

In a hospital environment in Kentucky, the chief administrator said that *"STAKEHOLDERS"* had eliminated the "it isn't my responsibility" syndrome throughout their entire organization. He enumerated any number of examples and closed with the observation that "now everyone is picking up trays."

The potential for positive culture change is unlimited. Maximizing an organization's potential, however, begins with its leadership believing that a significant untapped potential exists. It requires leadership to commit to educating everyone in the organization about business literacy, how the organization keeps score in reaching its goals, where it is going, and how each individual contributes to that journey.

Recognizing the Potential of People

At one time Andrew Carnegie shined shoes on street corners of New York City and slept in an alley. From that very humble beginning, he created a steel empire and became a great leader of industry. In later life he was questioned by a reporter: "Seems to me Mr. Carnegie, that the secret to your success is in the fact that you amassed this money at a very early time, and you learned early on that money makes money. It is like a snowball that runs downhill. Seems to me the secret to great financial success is simply being able to pool enough money early on."

Andrew Carnegie looked at his questioner and said: "You just don't understand. You could take away all my money, you can take away all my factories, you could even take away all our ways of doing things. You could take away everything, but leave me my people, and in five years I will have everything I have ever had and more beside."

Andrew Carnegie understood the prerequisite to creating value. It's good people who create value. It's the people who will invent the better idea, the better process, the improved tools. It is the people who will create and improve competitive advantage.

Mark Twain first told the story about a man who sought the identity of the greatest general who ever lived. In his search, the man was told that the person he sought had died and gone to heaven. At the pearly gates, he informed St. Peter of his quest, whereupon St. Peter pointed to a soul near by. "But that isn't the greatest of all generals," the searcher protested. "I knew that person when he lived on earth. He was only a cobbler." "I know," replied St. Peter, "but if he had been a general, he would have been the greatest of them all."

How many great generals do you have doing cobbler's work in your organization? How many great people never reach their potential because management doesn't have the belief that their people can contribute significantly more. Just as all employees have to have belief in their organization to maximize their contribution to their work environment, managers must truly believe in their employees' unlimited potential. Belief is a prerequisite to guide everyone toward a level of success that will maximize the organization's potential.

Earl Nightingale tells the story about a new teacher glancing over the roll book of her class on the first day of school. After each student's name there appeared a number such as 145, 138, 140, 147 and so on. The teacher thought to herself, "Look at those IQs.

I've got a terrific class." So she tried new methods and accelerated the course work. Her students responded exceptionally well to her creative approach. They worked harder and longer and received higher grades than any other group she had ever taught. It was only later that the teacher found out that the figures after the names were not IQs, but were each student's locker number. That story goes a long way toward proving that people will respond much according to what is expected of them.

The Importance of Knowing the Score

Management's misconception is that most employees understand where their organization is going and how they can contribute. It is too easy to overlook that the great majority of those working in our organizations simply do not know what the game is, or how we keep score. I often remember in this regard an afternoon outing some years ago.

I had just completed my military service and joined the Aluminum Company of America. Shortly after joining ALCOA, I participated in a six month product training tour. We visited all of ALCOA's plants in the eastern United States. There were six sales trainees involved in the training program: three from the United States and three from Aluminum Company of Australia.

Half way through the program, we were in Pittsburgh for a weekend. I invited the three Australians to go to their first baseball game on a day that could not have been more perfect. The sun was shining without a cloud in the sky and the temperature was about 70 degrees. The Pittsburgh pitcher was pitching a no-hit, no-run game through the seventh inning. It was time for a stretch. My Australian guests were really enjoying the day, and getting very enthusiastic about the pending Pittsburgh win, when Brian Day from Perth asked, "Michael, why don't they do anything about replacing that bloke throwing the ball? He doesn't seem to be able to hit the wood!"

How many people in your work environment don't understand how we play our game of business. If they have no idea about how the game is played, or how we score, how can they possibly contribute their true potential.

29

A study by economist Richard Freeman of Harvard and law professor Joel Rodgers of the University of Wisconsin concludes that the vast majority of our work force feels ignored in the workplace. There is a yearning among almost two-thirds of all employees to become more involved in contributing to the companies where they work. The same study also suggests that when paired with participatory management, quality circles and other forms of "employee involvement"—where workers have the opportunity to begin to think like owners—reward compensation can spur significant hikes in productivity.

Yet other studies have confirmed the finding that nearly 95% of all employees in the U.S. do not fully understand what their organization's priorities are, or how their work contributes to the achievement of those objectives.

For managers to have confidence that employees can make a much greater contribution by becoming involved, employees must be educated to understand how their company wins, how it keeps score, and what it is they can do to contribute as individuals and as part of a team.

Tapping Into Ownership Thinking

Skeptics question whether the complexity of *"STAKEHOLD-ERS"* concepts can be communicated to employees. The various experiences of companies implementing the methodology, however, show that participants readily grasp the essentials. It only takes good leadership. An example is the use of productivity ratios in our performance models. A productivity ratio easily translates into the concept that the more the company scores—that is, the more we grow without adding people or other unnecessary expense—the bigger the payout for everyone.

This simplistic approach to coaching stakeholders is an essential starting point, as illustrated in an example from the give-and-take during the first orientation when a healthcare institution was introducing the program to 400 of its 600 employees.

At the end of the presentation, the president asked if anyone had any questions. A new hire, entry level, non-exempt, just out of high school, raised his hand. He asked: "Does that productivity ratio mean if we can find ways of helping you identify unnecessary expenses that you will share those savings with all the employees?" The answer was, "Yes, that's right." With that the president asked if there were other questions.

But the young man didn't sit down. He continued on with his questioning. "Does that mean that if we started paying for our own coffee rather than the hospital paying for it, that you would share in the savings from that decreased cost?" Again the president answered in the affirmative and again looked to the others in the audience for additional questions. But the young man still wouldn't sit down. He said, "Well, how about this coffee situation? If we all agreed to pay for our own coffee, we would probably all use a lot less coffee and you would share those savings with us, is that correct?"

And the president again responded in the affirmative and congratulated the young man for his good example of how to increase productivity and share in the increased performance. The young man still didn't sit down. He then asked, "How much do we spend each year for coffee?" The president turned to the controller who replied, "In excess of $30,000 a year." The new hire then turned to his fellow employees and said, "I'll bet we would all vote to pay for our own coffee if we received a share of the increased savings. What do you think, everyone?" And everyone yelled, "Yea!"

Eighteen months later—without having the employees pay for their own coffee and following further orientation—the healthcare institution evolved from a negative cash flow to a very positive cash flow. (See Figure 3-2.) The three-year average of expenses-per-patient-day declined dramatically and salary expense per-adjusted-occupied-bed decreased 12.5% while the numbers of patients served and patient satisfaction improved beyond optimistic projections.

Figure 3-2 Comparisons: Before and After *"STAKEHOLDERS"*

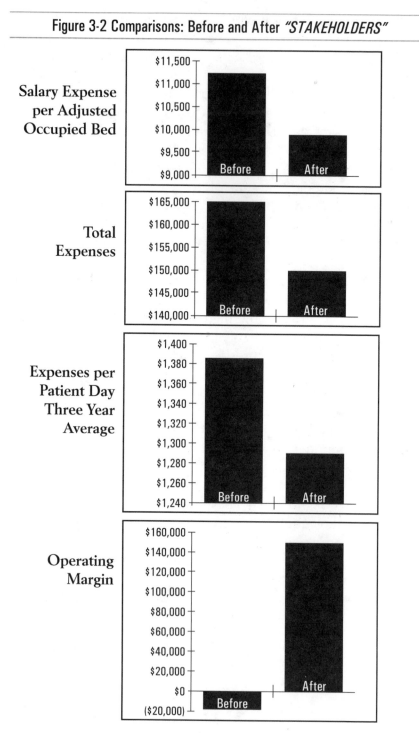

Salary Expense per Adjusted Occupied Bed

Total Expenses

Expenses per Patient Day Three Year Average

Operating Margin

"Who Needs Him?"

There are literally thousands of shared experiences to demonstrate the benefits of allowing people to think like owners.

One of the most timely and humorous experiences was in Kentucky. A small holding company operated two smaller independent companies with a similar product line in markets only six miles apart. The employees had all been coached that if the company could continue to grow and improve overall performance without adding unnecessary expense, the ownership would share in the savings just like the shareholders.

Eight months after "STAKEHOLDERS" was introduced, the president of one of the affiliate companies resigned to accept a CEO position with another company in a different state.

In a typical overreaction, the holding company management team scheduled a staff meeting early the following morning to calm the "leaderless" employees. They recognized their loss as a great opportunity for him, they wished him well, and then they assured every employee that recruiting a new president would be the holding company's #1 priority. They assured everyone that they would have new leadership within 3 to 6 months.

The holding company chairman barely got that commitment out of his mouth when it became apparent that the employees had a better idea. "Hey, we don't need a new president, we can operate very well without a president!" The employees suggested they could and would seek direction from the president of the nearby affiliate. The employees were right. The company realized significant savings that were shared with all stakeholders.

The holding company had operated on the assumption that they would always have a president at each affiliate. The employees knew better. They knew they could operate their satellite office just as effectively without the unnecessary expense.

That experience, by the way, reinforces a unanimous conclusion that management's greatest challenge after introducing "STAKEHOLDERS" will be to justify (unnecessary) expenses. What a great opportunity that will be for all stakeholders.

Having a relevant performance reward program not only gets everyone in the organization focused on the organization's strategic priorities, it also can do a lot for recruiting and retaining high performance people. A Florida company that did not have the *"STAKEHOLDERS"* methodology in place found they could no longer recruit people from a competing company that did have it. The people felt they would be giving up too much value, both short-term and long-term value, if they changed jobs.

"STAKEHOLDERS" concepts are complex; however, in implementing it, an organization interfaces the priorities it sets to a computer program that resolves the complex methodology. No less fundamental to successful implementation, however, is the necessity for the organization's leadership to believe in the capacity of employees to attain the new goals and to commit to helping them realize their potential.

Summary

The essence of success lies in creating an environment where everyone thinks and works like an owner. Then everyone understands the need and value in setting and striving for new goals beyond their present level of achievement.

Since 1990, companies of all sizes have incorporated *Performance Compensation for Stakeholders*™ to focus on a new combination of influences to manage performance. They recognize they must balance profit, growth, quality, and productivity in order for their organization and every individual within their organization to realize their full potential.

In accepting these influences as the key factors in achieving long-term shareholder value and tying these four influences to performance compensation, they have achieved levels of performance beyond anything they could ever have imagined.

New levels of success are being realized in environments everywhere. However, successful implementation of *"STAKEHOLDERS"* is bound up in the requirement for key managers and supervisors to recognize and tap the potential that exists within all of their people. It is the people who create the value, and it is the people who will create an improved competitive advantage.

Management's belief in the potential for greater achievement on the part of their employees must be accompanied by the realization that employees need to know where their organization is going, how it gets there and how they can contribute to that journey for new levels of achievement. Successful management will use *"STAKEHOLDERS"* to maximize human potential. This comes from ensuring that everyone in the organization learns how it keeps score, a prerequisite to empower them to work as stakeholders.

CHAPTER 4

Tenets for Maximizing Human Potential

"Organizations are not more effective
because they have better people.
They have better people because they
motivate to self development through
their standards, through their habits,
through their climate."
—PETER F. DRUCKER,
THE EFFECTIVE EXECUTIVE

Maximizing human potential is based on twelve prerequisite tenets that relate to expectations and standards of performance. The tenets are as follows:

1. Untapped Human Potential. One group of human behavior specialists concludes that the human being utilizes only 11% of their intellectual capacity. Another group takes great exception to those conclusions. Rather, they conclude that we humans use only 3% of our intellectual capacity in the contribution to our environment. Let's be optimistic and suggest people utilize 20% to 50% of their intellectual capacity. Think what they could contribute to their company or institution if they understood how the organization could maximize its potential and what they would receive from that significant improvement. Somewhere between 10% and 50% of capacity is sitting dormant. The untapped potential is there. The ultimate result of improving each individual's contribution lies in improving their understanding about what and how they can contribute, i.e., in improving the utilization of their intellectual capacity. That will not only benefit the organization, it will contribute to each individual's self-esteem, their job satisfaction, well being, their spirit, and their morale. It will create an enthusiasm about making a contribution.

One of the great stories that reinforces our untapped potential begins during the depression when a young Ph.D. candidate, George Johnson, majoring in mathematics, was about to graduate. There were no jobs for Ph.Ds, so he could see himself in the soup line. However, there was a rumor about that the person who received the highest marks in the mathematics final examination would be given a job as an assistant to the professor and stay on at Stanford. George Johnson was desperate! George tells the story.

"I worked and studied and studied and prepared, and prepared and concentrated so hard that when I came to the class for the test I was late. I ran to the desk and picked up the paper. It had eight problems, I solved all eight and then noticed that there were two additional problems on the board. I couldn't get one, so I switched to the other, and I couldn't do that, so I went back to the first. The bell rang. I said to the professor, 'There are a couple of problems that I didn't get done. May I have a little more time?' He said, 'Sure George, by 4 o'clock Friday, no later, put it on my desk.'

"I knew that there were students in that class who were smarter than I. And I knew that some of them would have all 10 problems solved. And here I was, stuck on two of them. But I knew that if somebody could solve them, why not me? I went to one and couldn't solve it, I went back to the other one and couldn't solve it. Day after day, night after night—Tuesday night, Wednesday night, Thursday. Finally, I solved one problem, but I couldn't solve the other one. I put the paper on the desk at 4 o'clock Friday. The professor wasn't there. I left. I was so depressed.

"I knew next week was the soup line. Saturday was black Saturday. Sunday morning, I will never forget it. About 7 A.M. I heard a loud pounding at my door. There was my professor.

"'George, George, you made mathematics history.' I shook my head and said, 'What do you mean?' He said, 'George, I was thinking as I came over here. You came late to class, didn't you?' I said, 'Yes, I'm sorry.' He said, 'No, no it's O.K. The eight problems were on my desk, you took them and solved them all. But the two problems on the board were not part of the test. George, I handed out the test paper and said to the class, 'The rest of your life, if you want to have a little fun with mathematics, keep playing with the two classical unsolvable problems.' And I put those on the blackboard. George, even Einstein to his death played with those two and couldn't solve them. You solved one. And I'm here to tell you that you have a job starting next week as my assistant.'"

George Johnson admits, "If I hadn't been late for that class, and if I had known, or heard him say, that they were unsolvable problems, do you think I would have solved them?"

People's untapped potential is beyond comprehension and it lies dormant in each and every one of us, waiting to be found.

2. Enthusiasm. People will become high performers only if they have reason to become enthusiastic about their workplace. Enthusiasm for the workplace is prerequisite for people to create the opportunity to realize their potential, that is, to become what they have the capacity and the desire to become.

3. Management's Responsibility. It is management's mission to create a working environment where people are as enthusiastic about coming to work in the morning as they are about going home in the evening.

4. Focus. Les Brown, a very talented, motivational speaker has noted that 'most people go through life *unthinkingly.*' He relates "unthinkingly" to driving home from work—all of a sudden you are in

39

your driveway and you don't even remember the time expended since you left the office because you have proceeded "unthinkingly." You arrive at a predetermined destination more as a *result of habit, than focus*. In order to maximize our potential, it is important to be consciously *aware of everything we do and to rid ourselves of the habitual unthinking process. We must always proceed with purpose*. Clarity of purpose is what focus is all about and it requires unrelenting focus by everyone in the organization.

The way to get people out of working "unthinkingly" is to give them direction and clarity of purpose. First, we must give them the focus, then meaning or purpose, and then convince them that they can make a significant difference.

5. *Making a Difference.* The vast majority of our workforce wants to make a difference. They want to make a significant contribution to their workplace. Unfortunately, the vast majority do not know how their organization keeps score. Stop and think about how your favorite athletic team would do if 85% of the team members didn't know how the team scored. Most employees have a clear understanding of their specific job responsibilities (function), but they have absolutely no idea what the company's priorities are, much less how they contribute to those priorities (results). Equally unfortunate, too many managers and supervisors do not have the confidence that their people have the intellectual capacity to understand how the company keeps score. That assumption is utter nonsense. The vast majority of the workforce has a significant capacity to understand and therefore could contribute much more if only they were taught the basics.

Too many people drift through life without knowing that they can make a significant difference. *It is management's responsibility to cut the drift*. It is management's responsibility to align and to educate, which is prerequisite to giving people the courage to dream, and to fulfill their dreams. If management will commit to that, the contribution to our organizations will expand exponentially. The key is convincing people that they have something significant to contribute and that they *can* make a difference.

It is management's responsibility to teach people how to make a difference. Many approach their day-to-day responsibilities unconsciously, operating moment to moment, morning to afternoon, day to day, week to week, in an unconscious state of mind. They are just getting the work done rather than focusing with a spirit of enthusiasm to find better ways to accomplish each task and to serve our customers.

As we pursue these ideas and issues, let's keep in mind that each and every individual in our world, in our country and in your company, has a talent, and within all that talent is untapped potential. If you are going to realize the potential of the area of work you manage, it is incumbent upon you—it is management's responsibility—to instill in each and every one of your people that they can do better, that they should do better, but more important, they deserve to do better! Furthermore, they deserve to share in the satisfaction and the value of making a greater contribution. Everyone wants to contribute, and they want to contribute significantly.

6. *Work Smarter, Not Harder.* It is very important to understand that we are not asking people to work longer or harder. We are only asking them to work smarter, by being focused and understanding how they can contribute to their environment.

7. *The Power of Empowerment.* There is one major external influence that will prevent an individual from realizing their dreams. That external influence is allowing someone else to define what it is they can accomplish. Other people's demands will impose limitations! That is why it is so critical to empower people to participate in the decision making process because people will consistently reach above the level of performance that is otherwise imposed on them. The key is to tell people what you expect them to accomplish, and then get out of the way.

8. *The Law of Contribution.* If we are going to help people realize their potential, and to realize what they actually can become, it is incumbent on all managers and supervisors to define why we are here in the first place. I believe we are here *to make a contribution to our environment, and then share in the reward of that contribution.*

9. *Senior Management Motivation.* Why is it that in most organizations the senior management team is most often the most highly motivated? It is because it is at the senior management level that most goals and action plans are established, understood, monitored—and, unfortunately, almost kept safeguarded. How enthusiastic and how motivated do you think your senior management team would be if they did not know what the company's goals were? How enthusiastic and how motivated do you think your senior management team would be if they did not know how the company kept score. That void is the source of all employees' untapped potential. Eliminating that void is the prerequisite to maximizing potential.

10. Goals. *Everyone deserves goals and* we do influence and direct our destiny through goals. This insight transcends all situations, all backgrounds and all conditions. So do the principles of thinking, feeling and behaving that evolve from it. The theme of this critical message is the need for *decisive goal-setting.* In order to maximize one's potential, it is necessary to set and know how to work toward personal goals as well as professional goals and to understand how one group of goals must support the other. Establishing goals and doing what it takes to reach them creates energy and enthusiasm. It reaffirms self-worth and gives meaning to life. Winners realize that success and satisfaction come from determining an action plan of positive self-direction. Winners turn dreams into goals. Winners follow their plan to achieve goals to turn imagination into reality. Winners have a game plan for life. Every winner I have ever met knows where he or she is going on a day-to-day basis, because winners are goal-oriented. They are self-directed to a wonderful and exciting road to self-fulfillment. We owe it to our people to understand the power and potential of their self-fulfillment.

Success has been defined as *the progressive realization of goals that are worthwhile to the individual and to other people.* If that is accurate, then people who are without goals are by definition incapable of being successful.

As we learn from this important message about decisive goal-setting, let us understand that the human system is goal-seeking by design. The entire process of human living can be compared to a homing torpedo or an automated pilot. If you set a target, an inherent self-activated system constantly monitors feedback from the target area, adjusts the course, and we become our own navigational computer. We inherently make every correction necessary to stay on target, i.e., to remain focused. If, however, we are not programmed, or we are improperly programmed, or we are aimed at a target that is too far out of our range, our homing device will continue to run until its propulsion system fails or until it self-destructs.

In 1955, there was a very important study in a well-known Eastern university graduating class. One of the questions in the survey was, "Do you have specific written personal goals, and do you have written action plans on how to achieve those goals?" Only 3% of that graduating class responded affirmatively, i.e., that they had written goals and specific written action plans on how to achieve those goals. Twenty-five years later that same graduating class was again surveyed. The survey dealt with success. Twenty-five years later the 3% of the graduating class that had written goals had accumulated 87% of that group's net worth. Although net worth is not the only measurement of success, it can certainly be an important reflection of success. Similar surveys have been conducted throughout the years and find that those people who have written goals with specific written action plans and implementation commitments consistently out-perform people who do not make that very important, yet not very time-consuming effort. What a difference!

11. Supervision. There are two basic supervisory work styles that influence performance.

- *developmental supervisors stimulate performance*
- *destructive supervisors inhibit performance*

Everyone prefers a developmental supervisor, regardless of their own values or the style of supervision they practice themselves. *Destructive supervisors* are generally insensitive to their propensity for quashing performance. They often even rate themselves on a par with *developmental supervisors*.

It is important to know that the ability to lead successfully depends on:

1) the individual leader's interpersonal competence,

2) the opportunity to work toward meaningful goals, and

3) the existence of appropriate management systems.

43

High-performance people consistently characterize their supervisors as people who are approachable, open-minded and maintain high expectations. They provide ready access to company information, encourage initiative and risk-taking and give credit for top performance. Low-performance people, on the other hand, more often describe their supervisor as authority-oriented and not usually receptive to conflicting ideas from subordinates. They tend to discourage initiative and are intolerant of mistakes. They tend to overlook successes and they stress failure.

12. The Right People. If *all* of your people, managers and supervisors, do not have a positive fit and commitment to upholding the previous eleven tenets, you likely have some people who would contribute more effectively in a different work environment. As you commit to high performance and significant reward for goal achievement, it will become very important to make difficult decisions about people who cannot get enthusiastic about their work and/or who would prefer not to be held accountable. They will become a real drag on your team's ability to achieve their potential, and they will create a cancer in your performance potential that will grow uncontrollably. Secondly, and equally important, if mediocre performance is tolerated, you are informing everyone that high performance is not appreciated around here, because what management does, speaks so loud that people never hear what is said.

As you prepare to lead your organization to exceptional performance, keep in mind that *if you have hired the right people, they will want to contribute*. They want to make a difference, and they deserve to share in the value of their contribution.

PART 2

Performance Compensation for Stakeholders Methodology

CHAPTER 5

Prerequisites, Assumptions and Pitfalls to Avoid

"Corporate performance is the result of combing planning and execution. It resembles a boat race. No matter how hard each crew member rows, if the coxswain doesn't choose the right direction, the crew can never hope to win. Even if the coxswain is a perfect navigator, you cannot win the race unless the rowers strive hard in unison."

—KENICHI OHMAE, THE MIND
OF THE STRATEGIST

A contemporary performance management system is very different from traditional reward programs. In evaluating whether or not they think that a more contemporary approach is the most appropriate way to reward performance, management must commit to a series of very important and difficult decisions based on prerequisite assumptions.

Prerequisites

Management must believe that:

1. Employees have a significant stake, a vested interest, in their organization's success. Their vested interest is actually greater than that of most shareholders. The employees' investment is their time and expertise, and more important, the financial security of their families. When employees understand that they have a very important investment, then they will want to learn everything they possibly can to help the overall organization to maximize its potential.

2. A *reward* compensation program should never put an employee's base salary at risk. Many compensation specialists recommend the opposite. However, placing base salary at risk will result in placing most employees' standard of living at risk. That is a negative incentive. Secondly, we want to have all employees think and work like owners. Typically, most shareholders do not have their standard of living at risk with stock ownership of *one* company, so why should the other stakeholders be required to put their standard of living at risk?

3. A *reward* program should not mean that anyone has to work longer or harder, they just have to work smarter. Therefore, everyone must be better informed. That is why the management team must believe that the organization's success is totally dependent upon everyone in the organization understanding what it is that we are trying to accomplish together. With that belief, management must then commit to teaching each participant how they contribute to that level of accomplishment.

4. There is a much better way to compensate people. First, everyone should receive a fair base salary and that salary should be competitive within the marketplace. The management team must also be committed to rewarding *everyone* in the organization for what all employees contribute together as a team. Everyone will have an equal opportunity to participate and everyone will have an equal opportunity to earn performance reward relative to their job, their performance and their base salary. Most important, the reward will be based on the same critical influences for management, supervisors and all other employees to ensure everyone is focused on the priorities the organization is trying to accomplish together.

5. The management team must recognize that everyone can make a significant contribution even though everyone's contribution will likely be different. They also must believe that everyone has a right to and deserves to share in a portion of what they can contribute to the organization. That requires every business unit to achieve a certain level of performance to justify base salaries, benefits and other overhead expenses. Just as with shareholders, the rationale is to share in the increased performance over and above what we call "baseline" performance. Every employee then shares the improved performance just as if every employee were a shareholder.

Pitfalls to Avoid

Too often, ill-conceived programs result in one or all of the following pitfalls that must be avoided. Successful programs avoid the following:

1. Avoid over-simplifying the system. Simple programs do not get the job done. Rewarding for performance entails a very complicated series of considerations; however, the program must be easy to administrate and equally important, easy to communicate to participants. That is why a successful reward program is complicated to construct.

2. Avoid limiting reward to sales performance. If the organization has truly committed to performance compensation as a part of its corporate culture, the reward program cannot be limited to sales. Rather, it should reward for all kinds of performance. The program should reward for sales as well as all work that *supports* sales. Customer contact or sales people are only successful if the people who support sales are successful in their commitment to excellence. Therefore, everyone must be in the loop to participate in the organization's reward for the achievement of quality business acquisition goals.

3. Avoid rewarding performance that would normally be achieved without incentives. An effective compensation program should reward for *improved* performance. Traditional programs too often reward results that would have been achieved without an incentive program. Some programs reward for more than the performance is worth, while others reward for selling rather than for improved sales performance. Also, when an organization pays for effort and activity instead of results, the allocation of reward pool for *improved* performance is diluted, and therefore is less effective.

4. Avoid asking the question, "What can we afford?" Beginning with a budget limitation will doom a reward program to failure. At best, an initial focus on budgeting reward will result in unnecessary restraints that will prevent the organization from maximizing its potential.

The biggest mistake an organization can make, and the one that puts the incentive program at risk, is to superficially analyze what the organization is trying to accomplish by installing a reward system. An in-depth critical analysis must come first. It must result in the establishment of minimum levels of expected performance. Reward begins after the minimum levels of performance are achieved. Then, the critical decision is to project what percentage of the *improved* performance should be allocated to the reward pool. This rationale precludes the need to "budget" for performance compensation.

5. Avoid beginning with an incentive program designed to reward individual performance. Beginning performance compensation programs at the individual level has very negative consequences. By the time all the incentive rewards are paid out, the organization is usually paying more in incentives than the overall performance is worth. This inequity is usually a result of ignoring that many people influence performance. Therefore, reward should first be given for overall team achievement.

6. Avoid creating internal competition and tension among employees. Too much internal competition encourages high achievers to run off by themselves without considering team or organization-wide goals. This can destroy the prerequisite sense of spirit among all participants which is necessary for an organization to maximize its potential. Too many individual incentive rewards can create divisiveness because the *emphasis* is on rewarding individual performance.

Individual reward is important, but the possibility of causing divisiveness is another reason why an organization must first stress organization-wide and/or team achievement before individual achievement. The emphasis on teamwork is very important. Always begin with team, group, or departmental rewards to build team spirit. Then, if appropriate, reward for individual performance.

7. Avoid arbitrary reward. An incentive reward pool must first be created by multiple corporate goal achievement and then allocated for pension, profit sharing, sales performance, productivity, and bonus. That is the only way to manage the total value of reward being distributed. It will also ensure that the value of performance compensation is not arbitrary and that it reconciles with a predetermined level of achievement value.

8. Avoid trying to build a reward system that is "fair to everyone." A worthwhile performance compensation program must begin with the premise that incentive programs cannot be universally fair. Everyone must have an opportunity to earn reward. However, various jobs and opportunities exist with differing levels of expertise and/or responsibility that help an organization achieve its goals in differing degrees. Therefore, an absolutely fair program will dilute the purpose of incentives so much that it will not mean anything to anyone. It is perfectly acceptable and occasionally necessary to offer different levels of incentive pay to employees in different areas of the organization. Assuring total fairness reinforces mediocrity, which is counter-productive to the very purpose of a reward program—promoting excellence.

The most important consideration to ensure that the program is *fair* is to have accurate measurement systems. There can be no tolerance for sloppy feedback or inaccuracy. The key is to communicate these "fairness assumptions" to everyone when the reward program is introduced.

Avoid rewarding for singular goal achievement, such as profit, or volume, or quality, or fee income.

There are two reasons for implementing multiple-goal, rather than single-goal, incentive models:

- Everyone's job responsibility includes all four influences. Therefore, reward should include all four influences.

- Rewarding one area of achievement, while ignoring other areas, invariably results in a de-emphasis of the latter.

For example, in a manufacturing operation when a reward system limits measurement to quality without consideration for volume, quality will improve dramatically, but the operation might experience production shortfalls that negatively impact profitability. If the emphasis is only on volume, quality will be ignored.

Another good example would be in banking, where lending officers are responsible for loan acquisition, loan quality, spread, fee income, as well as referrals of other products to other areas of the bank. If the program is limited to rewarding only new-loan volume, then loan quality, spread, fee income, and referrals will suffer dramatically.

10. Avoid designing a program without considering the actual contribution to the overall company goals. Often, inadequate measurement systems impose design limitations. A multi-billion-dollar company experienced this situation. Management was enthusiastic about the upward spiral in existing customer cross-sale ratios from less than 1.01 cross-sales per customer contact to well over 2.5 cross-sales per customer contact. However, management was perplexed because, during that same two-year period, profitable business grew at an unacceptable rate, much less than the rate of improvement in cross-sale ratios.

Investigation proved that the organization was paying rewards for cross-selling items that were not a priority and were not profitable. The reward program had too much emphasis on doing things right instead of focusing on doing the right things, i.e., concentrating on cross-selling rather than concentrating on profitable cross-selling. Reward must be for explicit but comprehensive objectives and based on increased value contribution to the organization.

The company eventually switched over to a measurement system that was far more comprehensive, flexible, practical, and less expensive to operate. Within months, people were emphasizing customer needs fulfillment consistent with the organization's priorities. Cross-sale ratios in profitable products remained high, while referrals in very profitable products grew at an astounding rate.

It is truly interesting how people will do what they are rewarded to do!

Even though measurement systems are important, a lack of measurement systems should never preclude installing a contemporary program. The time to begin is now, even if the only measurement system in place is the general ledger. Secondly, taking that initiative will help management identify and prioritize the measurement systems they need to measure and reward long-term performance efficiently and effectively. Too often, when management postpones the implementation of a reward program until they have created all the right measurement systems, they create the wrong measurement systems.

CHAPTER 6

Methodology: Performance Model Construction

*"Never send
a skinny person
for dessert."*
—AUTHOR UNKNOWN

Traditional incentive programs have been designed by very capable people with expertise in human resource administration, while traditional bonus programs have been influenced by the demands of Wall Street for short-term profit. Unfortunately, the people who have influenced traditional incentive and bonus programs have very little or no experience in managing a high performance company and/or no appreciation for the need to maximize long-term shareholder value. The time has come for business leaders to look elsewhere for direction. Performance compensation is a prerequisite issue for long-term success. Performance compensation programs, therefore, must be designed by people who have the experience and expertise to focus on the strategic priorities of the organization.

Traditional reward programs focus on the achievement of short-term priorities at the expense of long-term shareholder value. *"STAKEHOLDERS"* drives strategies that balance profit, growth, quality and productivity priorities to maximize long-term shareholder value, long-term viability of the company, and, therefore, long-term job security.

Implementing the *"STAKEHOLDERS"* system entails construction of a series of performance models that can be designed for every level of the organization. The models provide the quantitative infrastructure for carrying out the objectives discussed in earlier chapters.

The *"STAKEHOLDERS"* methodology is extremely complex. However, because the complexity is incorporated in a personal computer spreadsheet, the methodology is very simple to administer and, even more important, it is simple for all participants to understand.

Implementation begins with the process of building a series of models to define various levels of achievement. The results of implementation are communicated by the payout from a reward pool based on the organization's actual achievement of strategic priorities.

This chapter discusses how the organization-wide model is designed and how that model relates to the reward pool and ultimate payout of reward. Subsequent to building the organization-wide performance model, support models can be built for performance measurement and reward for division, department, branch, team and even individual performance reward.

Building the Organization-Wide Model

Building the organization model is the first step because it incorporates the set of performance levels the entire organization will strive to achieve. The model becomes the corporate focus, the scorecard against which everyone works in the coming year. It also becomes the basis for management's interim decision-making, and the model from which divisional, departmental, team and individual models are derived.

The model-building process entails eight steps based on management input and projections.

Step 1: Key Performance Indicators

Model building is usually based on an organization's existing three-year or five-year plan interpreted in terms of balancing growth with profit, quality and productivity priorities. As the first step in building the one-year model, management identifies the Key Performance Indicators (KPIs) within each priority that must be met in order to keep the organization on track toward achieving its strategic priorities. More specifically, the facilitator of the process would ask, "What key performance indicators must we focus on this year at the corporate level to ensure we achieve our strategic priorities and, therefore, maximize our potential over the next three to five years?"

Usually there are between seven and nine KPIs in a corporate model. They differ widely according to the type of organization using them. Often organizations do not have all of the appropriate measurement systems in place. For example, many companies are managing quality but are not capable of measuring the value of improved quality. All KPI values must be readily available from the general ledger or another type of measurement system, otherwise the KPI should be noted in the model as a *future measurement requirement*. This communicates to all participants that the KPI will become a part of the model just as soon as the measurement system is in place.

Growth KPIs for sales organizations are typically *total sales volume* or *sales volume by product line*; hospitals' growth issues would identify various *in-patient admissions* and *out-patient registrations*; while banks would focus on a breakdown of *loan and deposit volume*.

Profit KPIs always include various *margins* or *spread* and may also include other KPIs such as *miscellaneous income*.

Quality KPIs may include any variety of *service quality, product quality, returns, customer satisfaction, operational losses* or *charge-offs*, expressed in either a rating, the dollar value of quality improvement, a percent or in a ratio.

Productivity KPIs are presented as ratios and or as overhead expense. If a ratio is used, each model typically has only one productivity ratio that relates to a critical volume divided by an important category of expense. Some of the simplest productivity ratios are *pre-tax income* divided by *full-time employees*, or *sales volume* divided by *total overhead*. However, different companies have used more than 30 different corporate productivity ratios in various "*STAKEHOLDERS*" models.

Step 2: Setting Baseline Performance

The senior management team then establishes a baseline of achievement or minimum level of performance for each KPI. Baseline should be viewed as a level of achievement to justify base salaries and a level of performance to provide a minimum return to the shareholders. In the first year of using "*STAKEHOLDERS*," baseline is usually either the last year's actual results, the budget for next year, or a predetermined return on investment or return on assets. Very high performing companies use a combination of last year actual results and budget. In addition to serving as the basis for new performance goals, the baseline figures are an important training reference to teach everyone in the organization that we must achieve a minimum performance level, i.e., baseline, to justify salary and benefits before reward can be distributed.

Step 3: Maximizing Potential

Once baseline figures are established, management projects a series of hypothetical values (Column 5) that represent a maximization of the organization's potential during the first year use of the model.

Column 5 values should represent significant stretch, even ridiculously hopeful at best. Column 5 is a level of performance that can be achieved if everything happens that we plan to have happen, then we get lucky with some windfall, and nothing adverse happens during the year.

We assume Column 5 is unreachable. The premise here is that people will never achieve their maximum potential unless they reach for it. Secondly, in order to build a performance model with unlimited reward pay-out, people have to reach to performance levels that are theoretically unattainable. Experience has shown that people can achieve the unattainable if they set their sights on it, or conversely, will never achieve the impossible unless they focus on achieving the impossible.

Step 4: Calculating Intermediate Performance Levels

Potential levels of achievement between baseline and Column 5 must represent equal incremental increases between each level of achievement to ensure the methodology's mathematical integrity. A computer spreadsheet program can be used to subtract baseline from Column 5; divide that value by five levels of improvement, and then distribute the incremental improvement evenly to each column of achievement.

Step 5: Establishing Stretch Target Performance Levels and Below-Baseline Values

Most reward programs reward people only for improving performance, but rarely include a consequence for failing to achieve minimum levels of performance. This lack of "consequence" is perhaps the most important reason why people do not motivate themselves to achieve high performance.

Just as equal increments of improved performance levels of achievement are created above the baseline, the same equal increments for levels of performance fall below baseline. The rationale for demonstrating levels of performance below baseline is to teach everyone that the prerequisite to maximize an organization's potential is to balance profit with growth, quality and productivity. Therefore, if an organization achieves improved performance on one KPI such as growth by cutting price to achieve that growth, the stakeholders, just like the shareholders, would be rewarded for the value of the growth. However, the reward pool would be penalized for a predetermined portion of the decreased profit margin. Similarly, if profit and growth levels of performance were over baseline but the organization's quality deteriorated, the employees would be rewarded for their growth and profit levels of achievement. The reward pool would be penalized significantly for the deterioration of quality. Base salaries, however, are never penalized. Only the reward pool is penalized if any KPI achievement level falls below baseline.

Step 6: Weighting KPI Contribution

In traditional reward programs, various influences such as growth or margin are arbitrarily weighted. To share accuracy and mathematical integrity, all KPIs should be weighted mathematically, not arbitrarily. And, that mathematical weighting should be based on economic value created by the amount of stretch of each KPI. Therefore, weightings based on economic value improvement will then accurately communicate priority so that employees learn to focus upon the measures with the highest weighting because it leads to the biggest incentive reward.

Therefore, each KPI in *"STAKEHOLDERS"* is mathematically weighted. The weighting represents the relative value of each KPI achievement over baseline compared to the total value of all KPI contributions over baseline. KPI weighting is derived by dividing the pretax contribution of each KPI by the total contribution of all KPIs. The weighting communicates to both management and staff the KPIs most important to focus on in order to maximize the creation of value. For example, employees will soon demand to be taught how they can contribute to *profit margin* if it has the greatest weighting because it will have the greatest reward pool potential. Concurrently, employees will learn to understand that a *quality* KPI is very important, although it is weighted the lowest, because the low weighting communicates that *quality* issues in this company are so good that there is comparatively little value created by improving quality from baseline to (stretch) Column 5. However, there will be a prorated penalty to the reward pool *if* quality deteriorates.

The scorecard, then, becomes the corporate focus for everyone to make decisions, and from which performance reward is created.

Step 7: Calculating Reward Pool and Payout

The reward pool is created by a management team and/or board of director's decision to share a percentage of the improved value over and above baseline. Therefore, the reward pool is self-funding. The reward pool is typically presented in the model as a percent of salary.

Step 8: Trigger

This step produces a "trigger," which is typically shown in the lower left corner of the model. The trigger is the minimum level of performance that the organization must achieve before there is a reward payout. Typically, the corporate or total-organization trigger relates to net profit, pretax profit, return on assets, return on equity or return on investment. Subordinate models, for a division, department, branch group or team, also include a trigger relating to corporate profit. Subordinate models will often include additional triggers that communicate a requirement for a change of behavior or performance level before people within that subordinate business unit can qualify for participation in the payout in that respective model. Behavioral triggers might include standards for absenteeism, certification, business calls, service quality issues or a Personal Development Assessment (PDA) rating.

Reward Payout

It will become apparent that if a business unit achieves an identical level of performance (in the same column) for all KPIs—achieving all of Column 3, for example,—a reward pool of 25% of salaries will be created and distributed.

More often than not, however, an organization will not achieve the same performance level (column) for all KPIs. Instead, there will be multiple levels of achievement.

When a business unit achieves multiple levels of performance, a computer model creates the reward pool by multiplying the KPI weight times the corresponding reward pool.

The weighting factor for each KPI and the value of the reward pool for the column achieved creates the total reward pool.

Note that the failure to achieve the established baseline performance level—for example, the *profit margin* KPI—results in a deduction from the reward pool.

If a business unit creates a total reward pool of 6% of salaries, the reward pool for individuals with various base salaries is calculated as shown in Figure 6-1.

Figure 6-1—Reward Payout

Salaries		Reward %	Reward $
$15,000	X	6%	$ 900
$20,000	X	6%	$1,200
$25,000	X	6%	$1,500
$30,000	X	6%	$1,800
$35,000	X	6%	$2,100
$40,000	X	6%	$2,400

However, if the organization achieves on average a 20% reward pool as a percent of salaries, a reward pool would be distributed as in Figure 6-2.

Figure 6-2—Reward Payout

Salaries		Reward %	Reward $
$15,000	X	20%	$3,000
$20,000	X	20%	$4,000
$25,000	X	20%	$5,000
$30,000	X	20%	$6,000
$35,000	X	20%	$7,000
$40,000	X	20%	$8,000

The reward allocation is communicated to all participants as the breakdown for salaries between $15,000 and $40,000. This puts the focus on the lower-salaried personnel. It also implies that if an individual is making more than $40,000 they ought to be able to calculate it for themselves or they shouldn't be making $40,000 a year!

As an alternative to everyone receiving an equal percent of salary, reward allocation can be further divided by application of the PDA, which subjectively differentiates between high performers and low performers on various teams. For example, an exceptional performer who receives a high personal development assessment by their manager or supervisor could achieve 1 2 to 2 times the reward allocation. A low performer could achieve 2 of the reward allocated or even could be disqualified from participating in the reward pool if their PDA rated them below a minimum standard of expectation.

If the reward pool above was earned as a result of the total corporate model, each participant could also have access to an additional reward pool created by their own business unit and in some cases by their individual performance models.

Subordinate Models

Following the creation of the total-organization model, performance models for subordinate groups can be created for business and support units throughout the organization. Eventually, performance models can be created for team and individual levels of achievement.

Additional scorecards can be built to create "line-of-sight" between day-to-day activities, overall organization performance and the bottom line. Additional scorecards will improve an organization's level of business literacy, which is a prerequisite to maximizing performance that traditional profit-sharing, 401k, ESOPs and stock option plans fail to address.

The construction of subordinate models for divisions, departments or teams as well as individual performance models, begins with the question, "What key performance indicators are a priority to focus on at this level of responsibility in order for this (subordinate) business unit to support the senior business unit's ability to maximize its potential?" Then, just as in building the corporate model, each subordinate business unit constructs their models by identifying the KPIs. Then they establish baseline consistent with their senior business unit model and its stretch values.

Subordinate models will increase the organization's ability to more-accurately communicate its priorities by business unit. The more specific the model, the greater its value as a tool for educating everyone in the organization about what they can do to contribute to the performance of their team, department, division and, ultimately, to the total organization's level of performance.

The combination of subordinate performance models and the unique KPI and weightings provides employees with a more precise focus and understanding of where their efforts contribute, the relative reward for performance achievement, and the percentage of the reward pool that can be earned. Because all the influences and factors are known at the outset of the working year, as opposed to rewards being handed out arbitrarily after the fact, everyone becomes enthusiastic about the scoreboard and how to positively influence results.

Once the subordinate models are constructed, the contribution created by the sum of the subordinate models must equal the contribution of the senior model. We call this process reconciliation. It is a unique and prerequisite element of the *"STAKEHOLDERS"* methodology.

Reconciliation

The sum of the economic values created for each subordinate scorecard must equal the value created by the overall or corporate model scorecard. When the sum of the parts equals the whole (reconciliation), the company or institution can allocate the incentive pool on the basis of salary. This will provide everyone with the same incentive opportunity communicated and distributed as a percent of salary. Equally important, an acceptable level of profitability can be guaranteed no matter how much is paid out in incentive compensation. This seemingly minor technique will ensure that ownership and/or the board of directors will not make an arbitrary decision because the reward pool will be tied precisely to predetermined levels of the creation of value in pre-tax income. The key is that reward will always reconcile with performance and that reconciliation will be assured with the performance achieved at the corporate level as well as at each subordinate level.

Summary

The technical implementation of *"STAKEHOLDERS"* resides in a set of computer models summarized as spreadsheets. The models provide a quantitative infrastructure for carrying out *"STAKEHOLDERS"* objectives. They become the focus and scorecard for the total organization's and each business units' level of performance and reward distribution.

The models are built around strategic priorities to balance profit with growth, quality and productivity to ensure long-term shareholder value, long-term viability as a competitive organization and, therefore, long-term job security for all participants. Management sets a range of performance achievement levels for appropriate Key Performance Indicators that communicate a minimum level of expectation and the basis for the reward distribution. The methodology eliminates entitlement which contrasts with traditional methods of arbitrary reward. Everyone in the organization knows in advance the basis for reward, and, equally important, understands the implications of achievement levels below baseline, which cause the reward pool to be penalized.

CHAPTER 7

Allocation of Reward Pool and Deferred Compensation

The "*STAKEHOLDERS*" reward pool value can be distributed using a variety of instruments depending upon the strategic priorities of the organization and the preferences of each participant. To date reward pools have been distributed in:

Cash	ESOP	Retirement Programs	Annuities
Stock	401k	Phantom Stock	Stock Options

Some of the most successful companies utilizing the "*STAKE-HOLDERS*" methodology have offered a cafeteria option to allow each participant to choose any combination of three or four instruments for the distribution of their reward.

The advantages of employee choice are obvious. Individuals within any group of employees will likely have different personal financial priorities depending upon their age, family financial needs and net worth. Typically, young people prefer cash or cash-plus-stock or some other deferred reward. More mature workers will likely be looking for a greater allocation of their reward pool in a deferred instrument or allocated to their retirement program.

There are arguments against employee choice, but all are steeped in the bias created during the long-gone industrial economy—concern about employee's intellectual capacity to make good choices, paternalism and administrative cost/benefit. Advocates of employee choice understand and appreciate the untapped potential that exists among our knowledge workers and the power of empowerment. Most important, advocates of employee choice understand the importance of focus: "What *is* the primary objective of a reward for performance system? Is the primary objective to improve performance or to distribute value?" Traditional thinkers forget that the primary objective is to improve performance. That lack of focus has resulted in a quagmire of entitlements that must be destroyed before companies and institutions can begin to think about how to maximize their potential.

Allocating the Reward Pool

The chronological steps in creating and allocating the reward pool are as follows:

1. Determine the reward pool value for the accomplishment of baseline.

2. Calculate the net additional contribution to each additional column level of achievement.

3. Determine the percentage of improved performance per column that will be allocated to the reward pool.

4. Create the reward pool for each column level of achievement.

5. Convert the reward pool values to percent of salaries.

6. Determine the percentage of reward pool to be allocated to organization-wide goal achievement.

7. Allocate the balance of the organization-wide reward pool to the subordinate level of responsibility. (See Figure 7-1.)

Whenever three or four levels of reward pool are created, allocate the reward pool value from the divisional reward pools to departmental, group, team, and/or individual reward models.

Figure 7-1

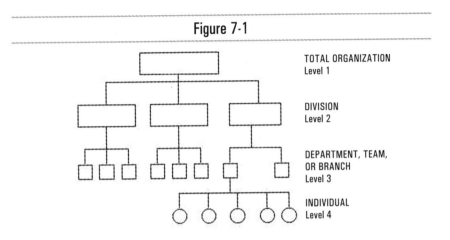

TOTAL ORGANIZATION
Level 1

DIVISION
Level 2

DEPARTMENT, TEAM,
OR BRANCH
Level 3

INDIVIDUAL
Level 4

Distribution Options

There are many distribution options for each pool or group of pools. The following discusses a series of options but the options are not limited to these examples. Rather, they are provided to demonstrate the flexibility of the methodology.

Following are seven alternatives for distributing reward pool on a percent-of-salaries basis.

1. Participation in One Model

		Achievement Levels Over Baseline				
Models	Baseline	1	2	3	4	5
Corporate Reward Pool	0%	6%	12%	18%	24%	30%

In this option, the assumption is that only one model is built for the entire organization and that all employees participate in the annual bonus distribution based on organization-wide goal achievement. In this example, nothing is distributed for Baseline. A range from 6% to 30% of salaries is distributed for achievement levels over Baseline.

2. Participation in Two Models

Models	Baseline	Achievement Levels Over Baseline				
		1	2	3	4	5
Reward Pool	0%	6%	12%	18%	24%	30%
Corporate Reward Pool	0%	3%	6%	9%	12%	15%
Divisional Reward Pool	0%	3%	6%	9%	12%	15%

In this option, everyone (except those at corporate headquarters who do not have a divisional or departmental model) participates in two models: a company-wide bonus and a divisional reward pool. The reward pool is evenly divided to allow 50% distribution for company-wide goal achievement and 50% distribution for each division's goal achievement. Those who do not participate in two performance models participate according to the *Total Reward Pool* levels of performance.

Therefore, if the company on average achieves Column 3 level of performance, the annual bonus distribution for people participating in two models will be of 9% of salaries for achieving Column 3 level of performance at the corporate level. If the organization has four divisions with one achieving Column 4, another Column 3, one that only achieves Baseline, and the fourth that achieves below Baseline, the payouts would be:

Division Achieving	Companywide Annual Bonus	Divisional Incentive Pool			Total Reward
Column 4	receives	9%	+	12% =	21%
Column 3	receives	9%	+	9% =	18%
Baseline	receives	9%	+	0% =	9%
Below Baseline	receives	0%	+	0% =	0%

In this example, the fourth division was a drag on the total organization as it did not even achieve minimum levels of expectation. Therefore, the division does not deserve to participate in

the company-wide payout of 9% and it did not qualify to participate in the divisional payout.

3. Participation in Three Models

Similarly, in this option employees participate in three reward
pools: an organization-wide annual bonus, a departmental, and an
individual model. The reward pools in this example are divided
equally.

		Achievement Levels Over Baseline				
Models	Baseline	1	2	3	4	5
Total Reward	0%	6%	12%	18%	24%	30%
Companywide Annual Bonus	0%	2%	4%	6%	8%	10%
Departmental Reward Pool	0%	2%	4%	6%	8%	10%
Individual Reward Pool	0%	2%	4%	6%	8%	10%

4. Participation in Four Models

In this option, employees participate in four models. The company-wide annual bonus pool for organization-wide achievement
is 0% for achievement of Baseline and a consistent 6% bonus for
achievement over Baseline. This allows a greater percentage of the
remaining pool to be allocated for departmental and individual
goal achievement.

		Achievement Levels Over Baseline				
Models	Baseline	1	2	3	4	5
Companywide Pool	0%	6%	12%	18%	24%	30%
Companywide Annual Bonus	0%	6%	6%	6%	6%	6%
Divisional Reward Pool	0%	0%	0%	0%	0%	0%
Departmental Reward Pool	0%	0%	6%	6%	8%	10%
Individual Reward Pool	0%	0%	0%	6%	10%	14%

There is no distribution for divisional achievement here; how-ever, divisional models must be created to establish parameters for constituent models, i.e., departmental and individual models. There is no distribution of reward for achievement of Baseline or Col-umn 1 in the departmental model and the distribution for achievement of Column 2 through Column 5 is shown above. This results in a greater portion of the pool remaining for allocation to individual achievement in Columns 3 through 5.

The allocation is created by what management deems is im-portant. Here the company wants company-wide achievement along with cooperation among all divisions and departments with the emphasis on each division and department working indepen-dently in support of corporate goals, and it places an even greater emphasis on exceptional individual performance.

This option and the next one are not recommended in the first three to four year's of a company's implementation of the "STAKE-HOLDERS" methodology as they are comparatively complex to introduce initially.

5. Varied Allocation

Another option for allocating reward pool as a percent of sala-ries is to allocate different percentages to various divisions, departments, and individuals. (See Figure 7-2.)

6. Equal Share: The most liberal distribution option

Every participant receives an equal share of the reward pool rather than a prorated share based on salary, no matter how many pools are created. This is the most liberal allocation of the reward pool because it distributes an equal share to every participant re-gardless of title, responsibility, or base salary. If an organization with 500 employees achieves goals resulting in the creation of a reward pool worth $500,000, each employee would receive a $1,000 bonus.

7. Tiered: Greater title receives a greater percentage of the reward pool

This option allocates a significantly higher percent of reward to those individuals with the highest base salaries and level of re-

Figure 7-2

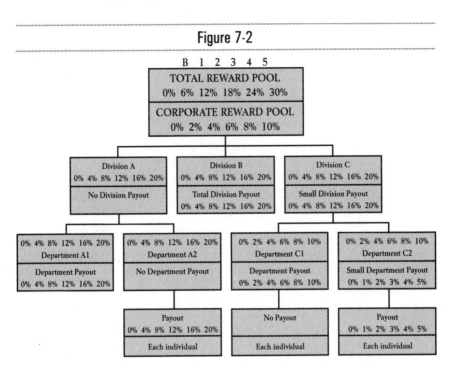

sponsibility. For example, the reward pool as percent of salaries might be as follows:

Models	Baseline	*Achievement Levels Over Baseline*				
		1	2	3	4	5
CEO	0%	50%	60%	70%	80%	100%
Direct Reports	0%	25%	30%	35%	40%	50%
Level 2 Drs	0%	10%	15%	17%	22%	30%
Other Exempts	0%	8%	10%	12%	14%	18%
Non Exempts	0%	4%	5%	6%	7%	9%

Converting Reward to Dollars

There also are many options for converting reward as a percent of salary to dollars. The most accurate is based on a percent of each participant's salary as it relates to total salaries. For example,

73

if a small company created only a corporate model and the level of achievement for each KPI was Column 3 and everyone in the company participated in the one model, the reward pool would be as follows:

Organization Achieves				Reward Pool to be Distributed
Column 3				$307,000
Salaries = $2.4 (m)				
Everyone receives				12.8% of salaries

Hence, an employee	Making		Reward %		Reward of
	$12,000	x	12.8%	=	$1,536.00
	$15,000	x	12.8%	=	$1,920.00
	$20,000	x	12.8%	=	$2,560.00

If another company achieved different levels of performance for each KPI, then the reward pool would be calculated as follows:

Organization Achieves	Column	Wtg.		Reward Pool	% of Salary
Sales Volume	5	34.8%	x	31.3%	0.1089
Gross Margin	4	29.3%	x	20.0%	0.0586
Inventory Audit	3	10.0%	x	12.8%	0.0128
Gross Margins/Payroll	2	26.0%	x	7.5%	0.0195
Incentive Pool		100.0%			19.98%
Everyone earns a bonus as a percent of salaries of					20.0%

Hence, an employee	Making		Reward %		Reward of
	$12,000	x	20.0%	=	$2,400.00
	$15,000	x	20.0%	=	$3,000.00
	$20,000	x	20.0%	=	$4,000.00

Distribution Methodology

The reward pool distribution can be made:

1. Annually in one lump sum,

2. Quarterly based on a 20-20-20-40% distribution, or

3. Monthly based on 8% of the projected annualized pool.

Whether the choice is monthly, quarterly or annual distribution, the staff needs and deserves to be informed of monthly progress toward goal achievement.

Monthly or quarterly distribution options provide for surplus accrual to protect against a subsequent period's level of achievement below baseline which would result in a negative penalty to the reward pool. If distribution is made monthly against annualized goals, the distribution should not exceed 9% of the annual pool. If distribution is made quarterly, the reward should be based on a quarterly allocation of 20% of the projected annualized pool in the first quarter, 20% in the second, 20% in the third, and 40% of the projected annualized reward pool in the fourth quarter. This will ensure a positive carry forward in the event baseline is not achieved in a subsequent quarter.

The distribution formula can be applied to all areas of the organization. If, however, a priority is placed on golden handcuffs, long-term goal achievement, or rewarding for quality asset acquisition, then a portion of the reward pool should be deferred.

Deferred Reward

The deferred reward program for management and other key employees has been created to ensure the organization achieves its two most important objectives.

- Maximize long-term shareholder value. Deferred reward will reinforce management's focus on and commitment to long-term strategic objectives.

- Retain talented executives and key players who are committed to leading the organization to exceptional long-term performance. Deferred reward creates the all-important golden handcuff.

75

The vehicle to accomplish these two objectives is the same *Performance Compensation for Stakeholders*™ corporate model that was created for the total organization, only we add *additional* reward pool for key executives. This additional reward may be deferred over a five-year period, although a shorter or longer deferral can be effective in certain environments.

We begin by utilizing the identical total organization model that was created for all employees. (See Figure 7-3.) We recommend that all employees including executives participate in the corporate pool created for all employees because we want everyone in the organization to understand that everyone is working toward and being rewarded on the same basis and for the same criteria, i.e., to balance profit with growth, quality and productivity.

Figure 7-3: Performance Compensation for *STAKEHOLDERS*™

Standard Corporate Model With Contribution Allocation

Achievement Below Baseline			Corporate KPIs	Achievement Levels Over Baseline				
-3	-2	-1	▓▓▓▓ Baseline	1	2	3	4	5
			Incentive Pool as a % of					
(10.4%)	(6.2%)	(3.1%)	Salaries	3.1%	6.2%	10.4%	13.9%	19.2%	28.1%

An additional deferred payout is created for those key executives and other personnel who have a major influence on decision-making resulting in long-term company results and for those personnel who should participate in a golden handcuff.

To the original model we add an additional reward pool for senior management and other key personnel. (See Figure 7-4.) In this example the board of directors has chosen to provide a two-tiered deferred reward pool for key executives. The chairman and

CEO participated in Tier 1 reward pool while two EVPs participated in Tier 2. Some companies have only one tier of deferred reward to ensure that all executives participate in the same pool, while other companies have created as many as four tiers for deferred reward compensation.

Figure 7-4: Performance Compensation for *STAKEHOLDERS*™

(Any Bank)
(City), (State)
Standard Bankwide Model

Achievement Below Baseline			Corporate KPIs		Achievement Levels Over Baseline				
-3	-2	-1	▓▓▓	Baseline	1	2	3	4	5
			Reward Pool						
(10.4%)	(6.2%)	(3.1%)	for Everyone	3.0%	6.2%	10.4%	13.9%	19.2%	28.1%
(15.0%)	(10%)	(5.0%)	Tier 1	5.0%	10%	15.0%	20.0%	25.0%	30.0%
(7.0%)	(5.0%)	(3.0%)	Tier 2	3.0%	5.0%	7.0%	9.0%	11.0%	13.0%

Let us assume that in the first year the organization achieves an average Column 4. A Column 4 level of achievement creates an annual distribution of reward for everyone in the organization who qualifies to participate. In this model, the annual payout would average 19.2% of all salaries. An additional reward of 25% of executives' salaries in Tier 1 would be deferred and an additional 11% of salaries would be deferred for the executives participating in Tier 2.

In this specific case study, the executives participating in Tier 1 would receive the 19.2% of all salaries at the end of the first year and an additional 25% of their salaries would be deferred over the subsequent five years. (See Figure 7-5.) The number of years the reward pool is deferred varies among companies.

Figure 7-5 Percent of Salaries in Reward Pool

Year	1	2	3	4	5	6
Tier 1	19.2%	5.0%	5.0%	5.0%	5.0%	5.0%

If in Year 2 the organization achieved even greater levels of improved performance—Column 5—the immediate annual payout would be 28.1% of salaries and the deferred reward for those in Tier 1 would be 30% of salaries deferred over the next five years. (See Figure 7-6.)

Figure 7-6 Percent of Salaries in the Reward

Year	1	2	3	4	5	6
%	19.2%	5.0%	5.0%	5.0%	5.0%	
Tier 1		28.1%	6.0%	6.0%	6.0%	6.0%

And if in the third year the organization achieved an even greater level of reward, there could be an immediate payout of 33.7% and a five-year deferred payout of 40% or 8.0% per year.

The golden handcuff is created very quickly after the second and third year when, in this case, there can be as much as 70-80% of salaries being deferred which would be forfeited if the participant left the organization.

Deferred Pool at Risk

If, however, in the fourth year the organization experiences negative results in the performance model, achieving on average Column B3, the fourth year annual payout would be a negative (15.0%). And if the deferred payout were put at risk against the penalty, reward due for Year 4 would result in a net payout of 4.0%.

This graphic demonstrates that the deferred compensation is at risk and that the model therefore model reinforces the need for key executives to make good decisions based on long-term results.

Figure 7-7

Year	1	2	3	4	5	6
1	19.2%	5.0%	5.0%	5.0%	5.0%	5.0%
2		28.1%	6.0%	6.0%	6.0%	6.0%
3			33.7%	8.0%	8.0%	8.0%
4				(15.0%)	N/A	N/A
Reward Due	19.2%	33.1%	44.7%	4.0%	To be determined	

Many companies put all deferred reward at risk; some companies do not. Others put some key managers' deferred reward pool at risk. The basis for the "at risk" decision is simply: "What are the company objectives for a deferred program? If the objective is to create a *golden handcuff* and only a *golden handcuff*, then the deferred compensation need not be put at risk. If the objective is to create a *golden handcuff and* ensure that executives are making decisions based on long-term results, then the deferred reward pool should be put at risk.

In addition, many companies have decided not to put the deferred reward pool at risk because the competition does not put deferred compensation at risk. However, the basis for that kind of thinking is again buried in the bias of traditional industrial economy mindset.

Cost of a Deferred Program

The following demonstrates the cost to shareholders for the deferred program. In year 1 the organization achieved Column 4 and created an annual payout of 19.2% of salaries and a deferred executive reward of

25.0% for Tier #1 Executives
11.0% for Tier #2 Executives

Figure 7-8 Performance Compensation for *STAKEHOLDERS*™

Corporate Model
DEFERRED Compensation

	Baseline	1	2	3	4	5
Tier 1: Reward Pool	$9600	$19,200	$28,800	$38,400	$48,000	$57,600
Salaries: .192m						
Deferred Reward as a % of Salaries:	5.00%	10.00%	15.00%	20.00%	25.00%	30.00%
Tier 2: Reward Pool	$4800	$8000	$11,200	$14,400	$17,600	$20,800
Salaries: .160m						
Deferred Reward as a % of Salaries:	3.00%	5.00%	7.00%	9.00%	11.00%	13.00%
Total Deferred $	$14,400	$27,200	$40,000	$52,800	$65,600	$78,400
Pretax Improvement (millions)	$.5165	$1.033	$1.550	$2.066	$2.583	$3.099
Deferred Reward as a % of Improvement in Pre Tax Income	2.79%	2.63%	2.58%	2.56%	2.54%	2.53%

For achieving Column 4...

Tier #1 deferred payout cost the shareholders	$48,000
Tier #2 deferred payout cost the shareholders	$17,600
For a total deferred cost of	$65,600

Since Column 4 created a pretax contribution of $2,583,000 over and above last year actual, the deferred reward only cost the shareholders $65,600/$2.583 million or 2.5% of the *improved* performance over last year actual.

Directors Rationale

The Director's Rationale (Figure 7-9) demonstrates the pretax income generated by each column, the cost of the *Deferred Program* plus the *Annual Bonus Payout*, the total *Bonus Pool*, the *Pre-tax*

Income after reward distribution, and *After-Tax Income* after reward distribution as well as *ROA* and *ROE* achieved per column **after** the reward payout.

Figure 7-9

DIRECTOR'S RATIONALE
PERFORMANCE COMPENSATION FOR STAKEHOLDERS

Corporate Model 2000 (millions)	Last Year Actual	Baseline	Achievement Levels Over Baseline 4	6	8	10
Pretax Income (m)	4.100	4.617	6.165	7.199	8.232	9.265
Pretax over Baseline (m)		0.517	2.065	3.099	4.132	5.165
% Allocated to Reward Pool		17.00%	19.00%	21.00%	23.00%	25.00%
Reward Pool (m)		0.088	0.392	.651	.950	1.291
Staff Salaries: $m 2.82						
Deferred as % Executive Salaries		3.1%	13.9%	23.1%	33.7%	45.8%
% of Improvement		2.79%	2.56%	2.53%	2.59%	2.63%
Reward Pool Deferred		0.014	0.053	0.078	0.107	0.136

Bankwide Model 2000 (Millions)			Achievement Levels Over Baseline 4	6	8	10
Pretax Income	4.100	4.617	6.165	7.199	8.232	9.265
Totals Allocated to:						
Executive Bonus (m) Deferred		0.014	0.053	0.078	0.107	0.136
Annual Bonus Payout		0.088	0.392	0.651	0.950	1.291
Total Bonus Pool (m)		0.102	0.445	0.729	1.057	1.427
+FICA @ 7.65% 0.0765		0.007	0.030	0.050	0.073	0.099
Total Bonus Pool + FICA (m)		0.109	0.475	0.779	1.130	1.526
Shareholders Value:						
Pretax Income (m):	4.100	4.508	5.690	6.420	7.102	7.739
Net Income with Tax Rate of: 40% 60.0%	2.460	2.705	3.414	3.852	4.261	4.644
Per Share Values						
Beginning Assets: ROA $244	1.01%	1.11%	1.40%	1.58%	1.75%	1.90%
Beginning Equity: ROE $20	12.3%	13.5%	17.1%	19.3%	21.3%	23.2%

In this particular case study the organization had created pretax income of $4.1 million last year and it budgeted a pre-tax baseline of $4,508,000 with a net income after tax of $2,705,000. The question for ownership and the board of directors is: "Would we be willing to share 17%-25% of the total improvement for all employees and an additional 2%-3% for deferred compensation for key personnel to take the organization from 1% *return on assets* to a 1.9% and a *return on equity* from 12.3% to 23.2%?"

Deferred Compensation for Other Key Employees

Deferred reward compensation for key employees is applicable in the following situations:

- To maximize long-term shareholder value (as deferred reward will reinforce decision-making based on long-term strategic objectives).
- To retain talented personnel (as deferred reward creates the all important golden handcuff).
- And/or, if results of the key employees cannot be measured on a 12-month basis. Examples of employees who cannot be measured in a 12-month period include bank loan officers, research and development specialists, design engineers and sales people where product profitability analysis does not compute to a 12-month time period.

Typically, employees who receive deferred reward participate in the annual distribution for earnings created by the total corporate model. Only their division, department and/or individual model earnings are deferred. For example, if an individual earned $5,000 from the corporate model and $10,000 from their subordinate models, they would receive the $5,000 for corporate achievement immediately. They would receive the $10,000 earned for their subordinate model performance over a period of time such as on a four-year 20%-20%-20%-40% distribution basis. If a manager earned $5,000 from the corporate model and an additional $10,000 from their departmental model, they would receive the $5,000 and 20% of their department and individual model earnings immediately.

Mathematical Integrity

The mathematical integrity of the model will allow for a very accurate multiple-model payout.

For example, if there is a total or overall reward opportunity of from 5% to 40% and there are two levels of reward distribution, the reward pool can be allocated 50% to corporate-wide achievement and 50% to the second level or subordinate level of performance. (See Figure 7-10.)

Figure 7-10 Multi-Model Payout Example...

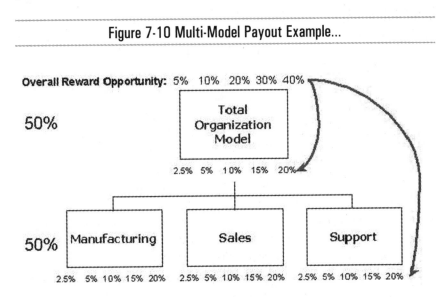

For example, if the total organization achieved on average Column 3, everyone who was participating in two levels of performance reward would receive 10% of salary as a reward for their contribution to the corporate level of achievement. Then, if one of the subordinate units achieved on average Column 2 level of performance, they would get an additional 5% reward, yielding a total reward pool for participants in that business unit of 15% of salary. When the middle unit achieved Column 3 they would receive 10% for their contribution for corporate and an additional 10% for their contribution to their business unit. The third business unit would receive 10% for their contribution for corporate plus 15% for their contribution to their business unit.

This provides for a very unusual catalyst to eliminate "this is not my responsibility" syndrome. For example (Figure 7-11), suppose the unit on the right found themselves in early mid-year projecting a Column 4 payout of 15% for their business unit but could accurately conclude there was no way they could improve performance beyond Column 4 because of outside influences, turns in the market or whatever. The participants in that business unit will learn very early on that the only way they can help themselves improve their reward is by helping everyone in the other business units as best they can to improve the performance of those units. That way, the overall performance in the corporate model could improve from Column 3 to Column 4 and everyone would then get an additional payout. This catalyst for everyone to work towards teamwork is unique. It is very apparent to all participants because of the way the subordinate models reconcile with overall performance and the subordinate reward pool always reconciles with the reward pool created at the corporate level.

Figure 7-11 Multi-Model Payout Example...

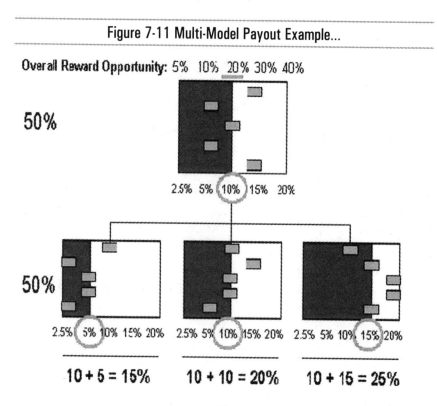

Overall Reward Opportunity: 5% 10% 20% 30% 40%

50%

2.5% 5% (10%) 15% 20%

50%

2.5% (5%)10% 15% 20%   2.5% 5% (10%) 15% 20%   2.5% 5% 10% (15%) 20%

10 + 5 = 15%   10 + 10 = 20%   10 + 15 = 25%

You will also note that whether you participate only in the corporate model with a reward opportunity of 5-40% or participate in two levels of performance where portions of the reward pool are allocated to the subordinate level of performance, everyone always has the same opportunity for reward pool. (See Figure 7-12.)

Figure 7-12 Multi-Model Payout Example...

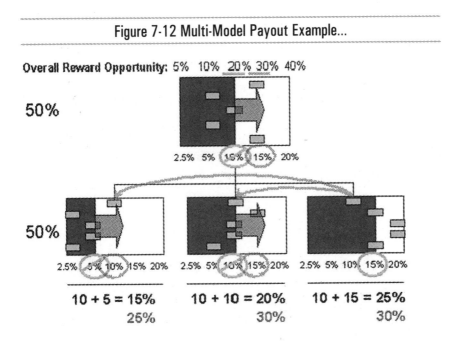

As with any great opportunity, there are always advantages and disadvantages. For people in this particular organization who only participate in the corporate model (for example people at headquarters or at holding company) the opportunity advantage is that they will always receive the average reward pool created by the performance of the total organization. Their disadvantage is that people participating in two or more business units for reward pool will have the opportunity of contributing and being rewarded for greater than the average of the corporate reward pool. However those people have a disadvantage in the risk of participating in a business unit that achieves less than the average of corporate performance and therefore a total reward pool that is less than the average paid out of corporate level.

The allocation of the total reward pool to the subordinate levels depends upon what the organization is trying to accomplish. Again, what are the strategic priorities? If there is a priority to create more teamwork among the subordinate business units, then more of the total reward pool should be allocated for corporate-wide achievement and less to subordinate levels. If, however, the strategic priorities are to put more emphasis on subordinate model results, then a greater portion of the total reward pool should be allocated to the subordinate models.

A couple of excellent examples were experienced in a company with one retail business unit in Nevada, another retail business unit in Northern California and a wholesale distribution unit in Southern California. There was obviously very little opportunity for synergy between the subordinate business units. Therefore, the headquarters allocated 20% of the total reward pool for overall corporate level of achievement and 80% of the reward pool for levels of performance at the subordinate level. Then, as the subordinate business units built models for their departments and divisions, they distributed the 80% of reward pool evenly between the overall business unit and the departments and divisions within each business unit.

Allocation Option via Personal Development Assessment

Many companies build individual performance models for sales people, tellers and customer service personnel. Instead of creating performance models for individual employees, many companies allocate reward to individual performers using the Personal Development Assessment (PDA) (Appendix V) as a basis for reward allocation to ensure that the higher-performing members in a department or team receive a greater payout than lesser-performing team members.

The PDA will replace traditional annual reviews for two very important reasons. First, traditional annual reviews are often negative, ill-planned and ill-thought-out, and often postponed for all kinds of reasons including that annual reviews are typically not a positive experience for anyone participating. Secondly, in the information society driven by knowledge workers, the paternal implications of "review" must be re-placed by the positive developmental implications of a PDA.

Methodology

There are at least five rating categories in a typical PDA, and each category can be broken down into various elements:

1. Job performance
- Job knowledge
- Job skill
- Quality
- Work speed
- Policy compliance

2. Communication
- Responsiveness to requests
- Responsiveness to feedback, written, oral, external

3. Interpersonal skills
- Attitude cooperation
- Team player
- Integrity
- Adaptability/creativity
- Judgment/maturity
- Initiative/intensity

4. Participation
- Meetings
- Teams
- Training
- Attendance/tardiness
- Notification of absence

5. Contribution to "*STAKEHOLDERS*"
- KPIs
- Model basics
- Status report meetings
- Action plans

6. Other categories unique to the company of department

A rating scale guides the employee and supervisor/manager in evaluating and rating each participant. (See Figure 7-13.)

Figure 7-13

A scale guides the employee and supervisor/manager
in evaluating and rating each participant.

Needs Improvement		Meets Expectations	Exceeds Expectations	
NMI—Needs Major Improvement (Rating = 1)	NSI—Needs Some Improvement (Rating = 2)	ME—Meets Expectations (Rating = 3)	EE—Exceeds Expectations (Rating = 4)	SEE—Substantially Exceeds Expectations (Rating = 4)
Must provide **SPECIFIC EXAMPLES** of individual behaviors to support rating of NSI or NMI			Must provide **SPECIFIC EXAMPLES** of individual behaviors to support rating of EE or SEE	
Must create a **PERSONAL ACTION PLAN** to improve performance				

The assessment must be started and finished in less than two weeks.

It is recommended that *every individual* in an organization complete a PDA at least once every quarter with the overall score for the year calculated as the average of each PDA score. There may be some resistance to the frequency of Personal Development Assessment; however, managers have no other priority that is greater than developing their people. Proponents of frequency understand that it is a prerequisite to achieving high performance in any organization. If people resist because "I don't have time," they are really saying that they do not care, because personal development of every individual in the organization should be priority #1 among all managers and supervisors. Secondly, consider that the investment of their time is somewhere between two and four percent of most managers' time in their total work year (See Figure 7-14.)

Figure 7-14

Suppose...	Suppose...
One Manager has 13 staff.	One manager has 6.5 staff.
There are 13 weeks in a quarter.	There are 13 weeks in a quarter.
Completing 1 review per week will consume approximately 1.5 hours (30-45 min. for review, 30-45 min. for meeting).	Completing 1 review every other week will consume approximately 1.5 hours (30-45 min. for review, 30-45 min. for meeting).
There are 40 hours in a work week.	There are 80 hours in two work weeks.
1.5/40.0 = **3.8%** of manager's time spent on staff development.	1.5/80.0 = **1.9%** of manager's time spent on staff development.

One of the primary responsibilities of any manager is staff development!

Scoring System

The scoring of Personal Development Assessment is as follows:

Figure 7-15 Scoring System (Example)...

Rating	Points		# of Ratings		Score
SEE	5.00	X	2	=	10.00
EE	4.00	X	5	=	20.00
ME	3.00	X	15	=	45.00
NSI	2.00	X	5	=	10.00
NMI	1.00	X	0	=	0.00
Total			**27**		**85.00**

Weighted Average Rating: 85.00 / 27 = 3.15

And there is an option to create a reward-pool multiplier to apply to the *"STAKEHOLDERS"* allocation of reward pool:

Figure 7-16 Optional: Reward Pool Multiplier...

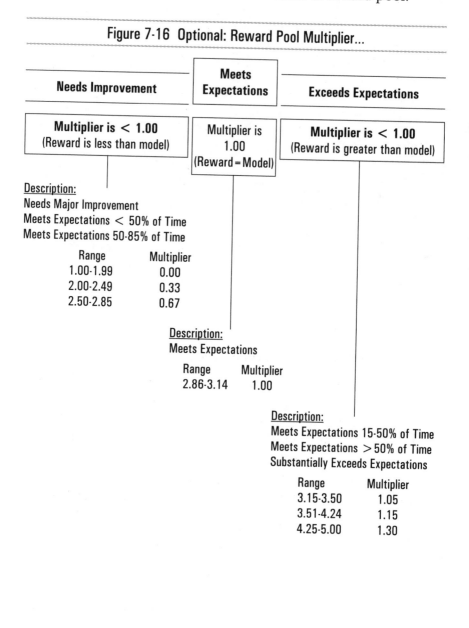

Needs Improvement	Meets Expectations	Exceeds Expectations
Multiplier is < 1.00 (Reward is less than model)	Multiplier is 1.00 (Reward = Model)	**Multiplier is < 1.00** (Reward is greater than model)

Description:
Needs Major Improvement
Meets Expectations < 50% of Time
Meets Expectations 50-85% of Time

Range	Multiplier
1.00-1.99	0.00
2.00-2.49	0.33
2.50-2.85	0.67

Description:
Meets Expectations

Range	Multiplier
2.86-3.14	1.00

Description:
Meets Expectations 15-50% of Time
Meets Expectations > 50% of Time
Substantially Exceeds Expectations

Range	Multiplier
3.15-3.50	1.05
3.51-4.24	1.15
4.25-5.00	1.30

Examples of pool payouts would be as follows:

Figure 7-17 Payout Examples...

	Avg Rating	Multiplier		Reward Pool		Reward
Helen "High Performer"	4.30	1.30	x	10.0%	=	13.0%
Marty "Meets Expectations"	3.05	1.00	x	10.0%	=	10.0%
Ned "Needs Improvement"	2.40	0.33	x	10.0%	=	3.3%

Policy for Change in Employment Status

The following is a recommended policy relative to change in employment status and to deferred compensation. This policy should be reviewed and finalized by the organization's legal counsel. Their findings and recommendations should then be documented as part of the organization's personnel policy.

1. Voluntary resignation during plan period.
   RESULT: Loss of eligibility for any portion of the plan.

2. Involuntary termination for cause.
   RESULT: Loss of eligibility for any portion of the plan. Cause must be documented in the employee's personnel file.

3. Transfer, demotion, promotion.
   RESULT: Maintain eligibility for pro-rated reward payable at the end of the plan period.

4. Approved leave-of-absence.
   RESULT: Maintain eligibility for pro-rated reward payable at

the end of the plan period or upon return to active work, whichever occurs later.

5. Retirement
RESULT: Maintain eligibility for pro-rated reward payable at the end of the plan period.

6. Death
RESULT: The estate would maintain eligibility for pro-rated reward payable at the end of the plan period.

Note: Pro-rated reward payouts are calculated according to the number of completed quarters a participant was in the plan.

Summary

The viability of a performance compensation program depends on its ability to flexibly respond to an organization's cultural demands and priorities. How a reward pool is allocated is prerequisite for success. Secondly, and equally important, a deferred reward package for key employees is paramount to the overall focus on long-term shareholder value and the retention (golden handcuff) of the most important personnel.

CHAPTER 8

Coaching
STAKEHOLDERS™

> *"The mind stretched to a new idea never*
> *goes back to its original dimensions."*
> —OLIVER WENDELL HOLMES

Coaching stakeholders is prerequisite for success. Therefore, how and when the coaching techniques are presented is critical.

In a survey of over 300 companies who had used the methodology for at least three years, CEOs were asked to relate how successful the program had been in improving performance for their organization. The survey included questions to determine how results were communicated to the workforce in the *"STAKEHOLDERS"* monthly status report meetings, how the organization used the recommended agendas for each coaching and status report meeting, and if all the managers and supervisors had been trained in the use of the *"STAKEHOLDERS"* coaching materials. The survey results were overwhelmingly positive. (See Figure 8-1.)

Figure 8-1 *"STAKEHOLDERS"* CRITERIA FOR SUCCESS

Response to Survey

% OF CLIENTS	MATERIALS & TRAINING IN USE	SUCCESS RATING
60%	Scheduled monthly status report meetings with recommended agendas and using coaching materials	Highly Successful
30%	Scheduled monthly status report meetings without recommended agendas and managers had not been introduced to the "Coaching *STAKEHOLDERS"* materials.	Moderately Successful
10%	No monthly status report meetings	Unsatisfied

Over 60% of the management teams were systematically scheduling and facilitating monthly status report meetings. They used the recommended coaching agendas and their managers and supervisors had been trained on how to use the coaching materials. Those 60% concluded that *"STAKEHOLDERS"* proved highly successful as it significantly improved their companies' performance.

Approximately 30% of the responding participants related that they did schedule monthly status report meetings, but they did not use the recommended agendas and their managers and supervisors had not been exposed to the "Coaching *STAKEHOLDERS"* training materials. Rather, they continued with their traditional method of communicating to employees with boring, top-down report sessions without encouraging participation from their audience. Those 30% concluded that the program had a moderate influence on their company's success. Subsequent to the results of the survey, the 30% made a new commitment to "coaching" and improved their performance substantially.

Less than 10% of the respondents reported that they had not been as successful using the *"STAKEHOLDERS"* program as they had hoped to be. Their response further related that they had never had monthly status report meetings, and their managers and supervisors had never been introduced to the "Coaching *STAKEHOLDERS"* training materials. "We didn't have the time" was the excuse of every management team that did not commit to *"STAKEHOLDERS."* No wonder they were not successful.

"STAKEHOLDERS" is a personnel development program based on improving communications throughout the entire organization. A management team must find the time to improve and increase communications throughout the entire organization in order to maximize potential. The prerequisite is coaching.

Coaching Defined

Coaching is a systematic focus on the development of human potential. It is a process to reinforce belief in the values and the vision of the organization to enable focused goal-setting and strategic actions in order to realize extraordinary results. The roll of the coach is to improve and maximize results by working with and through other employees to produce clarity, focus, responsibility and a workplace environment that energizes people to maximize their potential.

Coaching is uniquely different from training, mentoring, managing, and performance correction.

Training typically reinforces traditional organizational top-down direction and decision-making and therefore it creates an environment of dependency. It usually does not take into consideration people's existing skills, motivation, or commitment, and therefore it does not usually result in radical shifts in people's thinking and actions. Rather, training is more a means of delivering a structured course of study to improve a set of skills.

Mentoring is also a top-down experience. It is a positive one, but one that is limited to one individual passing on knowledge and experience to a novice. Mentoring is very informal and more often than not is focused on career advancement. Too often, mentoring fosters dependency on both the mentor and the individual. Again, mentoring tends to reinforce traditional organization structure and top-down processes.

Managing has been defined as a process to control action, use, or work process, another top-down approach. Professional managing results in getting another person to do what a superior wishes. It also has implications of contriving to get along.

Performance correction is a negative management process that deals with undesirable or unacceptable behavior and with levels of performance that fall below established standards. It attempts to resolve behavior or attitude problems. It is not collaborative nor is it interdevelopmental, and, again, it is hierarchical in its orientation.

Coaching enhances. It complements traditional process improvement programs because it adds the all-important and prerequisite interpersonal factors to the traditional focus on tools, techniques and work processes. The overriding additive that coaching brings to traditional improvement programs is participatory interaction focused by a structure for measurement of quantifiable results.

The business environment is experiencing a period of profound transition marked by changes such as the emergence of the knowledge worker as a key element of the workforce. Such changes are more radical and occurring more rapidly than at any other time in history. These changes require traditional managers to examine the basic assumptions about business reality because the old assumptions about reality are no longer relevant.

The idea that employees must be managed is finally experiencing its death knell. Rather, knowledge workers must be led. Knowledge workers demand more information and they deserve it. Equally important, shareholders deserve assurance that their management team will take advantage of this significant but untapped resource. The prerequisite is coaching.

Coaching will clarify the invaluable awareness, reinforcement and belief that must underlie the work of all employees. A commitment to coaching will transform the workplace from one where people are subordinate and receive direction from others to one where stakeholders commit to doing what they care passionately about. Everyone wins—all stakeholders, the workforce, the management, the leadership, the shareholders; and the customer will benefit most of all. Then, and only then, will organizations achieve significant competitive advantage.

Successful organizations will respond to these demands with a continued commitment to improve knowledge within their cultures. To do this, leaders and participants alike, all stakeholders, must radically shift the way they think and act in relationship to work. They must place a new emphasis on learning. They must learn how to take advantage of the collective potential of knowledge workers. This will require a new type of workplace relationship. Coaching provides both a technology and process for such a relationship and therefore will become the foundation stone for successful organizational transformation to maximize potential. Traditional status report meetings have lecture, top-down and hierarchical reporting with very little if any feedback. These traditional meetings typically end with the unanswerable "Are there any questions?"

Rather, the coaching methodology seeks input from everyone in the organization recognizing that people are the most significant resource in creating optimal strategies to pursue and achieve goals. The process includes defining the priorities, designing the work or action plans, writing those action plans down for commitment, allocating responsibility for fulfilling the action plans, and establishing a deadline for accomplishment.

Consistent feedback is also prerequisite. Feedback is the lifeblood of the coaching process no matter what the business size. There is a need to continually express where the organization is going, where it is at this time, what we are doing right and what must be done differently to improve what we are trying to accomplish together.

Prerequisites

The transformation to a coaching-based organization requires commitment and sustained sponsorship at all levels of the organization. Not everyone will make that commitment simultaneously. As we will discuss in Chapter 11 on *Managing Change*, the process can be unsettling to an organization's culture because the process encourages the development of personal leadership throughout the organization, not just top down or hierarchical. This transformation can be difficult for those who remain tied to a traditional organizational structure.

Invariably, there will be organization members who are reluctant to enter into a coaching relationship due to internal or personal obstacles. Moreover, coaching is not a quick-fix program for serious, organizational and individual performance problems. Finally, those organizations that enjoy protected market niches may not have a compelling need or desire to introduce coaching as a vehicle for transformation. The pain of retaining the status quo is not (yet) great enough.

Not everyone can be a coach or be coached. Typically, between 1% and 6% of individuals are not coachable. In environments where the corporate culture is more negative than positive, the percentage of uncoachables can be much higher.

There are several reasons why people are not coachable. They may not want to be coached because they are vested in the traditional ways. Or they are unwilling. They may have serious performance problems and therefore may feel threatened by being held accountable. Others may be planning to retire soon or move to another job. However, as an organization begins its transformation, uncoachable individuals will likely seek a different workplace because the standards are being raised and the organizational culture expectations are greater for everyone. The pivotal issue is accountability.

When more than one hundred CEOs of coaching-based organizations were asked if they would ever consider re-hiring an individual who terminated employment because of the company's transformation to high expectations and accountability, the answer was consistently: "Never!" When asked if the company hired personnel to replace those who terminated due to the new standards, the response was consistently: "Rarely!" Enough said for the value of people who do not want to be coached and be held accountable.

The even better news is that work environments with emphasis on accountability invariably attract and retain high-caliber talent.

All progressive-thinking managers will welcome the paradigm shifts. Their new and additional responsibilities as coaches will serve as a catalyst to develop focus on results, rather than just managing activity. They will learn to empower individuals to take more-effective actions rather than to control them. They will create an environment where the theme is "let's don't just do things right, let's do the right things right." They will eliminate the "it isn't my responsibility" syndrome. Coaching will focus alignment rather than using pressure to motivate. It wills collaboration and planning rather than management by crisis. The overall theme will be "how can I support you" rather than "remember that you report to me."

There are significant differences between traditional and coaching-based organizations. (See Figure 8-2.)

Figure 8-2 Comparison Of Traditional And Coaching-Based Organizations[1]

TRADITIONAL ORGANIZATION	COACHING ORGANIZATION
Top-down decision-making	Multi-level decision-making
Incremental learning leading to incremental improvement in products and services	Transformational learning leading to product and service innovation
Bureaucracy and management control systems	Organizational support systems
Segmented, vertically organized structure with explicitly defined job responsibilities	Cross-functional teams, horizontally organized or matrix structures with loosely defined responsibilities
Performance measured against top-down goals, usually with limited commitment by employees	Performance measured against shared goals with strong personal commitment by organizational members
Organizational leaders planning, directing and reacting	Organizational leaders supporting, informing and influencing
Career growth measured by promotion relationships that are competitive	Career growth measured by depth and breadth of expertise and strength of partnerships/networks
Organizational culture promoting employee dependence and entitlement	Organizational culture promoting interdependence and self-reliance of members

Leadership Coaching Style

The best coaches are those who express a high level of consideration for their stakeholders and who set very clear achievable goals with them. Successful coaches ensure that everyone in the organization has personal goals tied to the overall goals of the business unit.

Successful coaches demonstrate what they stand for and what they expect of their stakeholders. They provide positive encouragement and praise and reinforce everyone on the team in a positive way.

The clear standards of performance expectations will allow all stakeholders to gauge their level of achievement. It is the basis for the *"STAKEHOLDERS"* program that all employees know how their business unit and the total company keep score, and what it is that each person must focus on and learn to do in order to score well above the norm.

However, over 90% of the workforce does not understand what operating margin is, much less how they contribute to it. If personal goals must be tied to overall corporate and departmental business unit goals, then each participant must first understand how their business unit creates value.

It sounds elementary, and it is elementary, but if stakeholders do not know how their team keeps score, they cannot possibly know how they can personally contribute and they cannot measure their own performance relative to that score. This huge void in understanding is a result of the traditional focus on function or activity rather than results.

Secondly, and equally important, if the workforce does not understand how their company or business unit creates value, there is no way any one individual, much less the entire team, can realize his or her full potential. It begins with understanding how value is created and how each individual contributes to the value being created. That begins with understanding, or business literacy, about profit.

Profit With Honor

In biblical times, it was said that a prophet was without honor in his own home. Our contemporary business environment has created a situation in which profit is without honor among the workforce, in the media, and throughout academia. Why? How can so many good people be so ill informed?

How many times in the last decade as America rebuilt its economy to be efficient—to be competitive again—did the media blast management for sacrificing the workforce for the sake of profit? How many thousands of times has academia reinforced that mindless nonsense in the classroom? And what about the workforce? Why do they not understand that profit creates jobs and financial opportunity while inefficiencies destroy jobs and their own financial opportunity? Can you imagine what kind of U.S. economy we would be experiencing today if its leadership had not made the tough decisions of the late 1980s and early 1990s.

This crusade against profit is totally irrational. Unfortunately, the crusade is fueled by the very human condition it attacks: greed. Selfish interests out to create power, wealth or influence are what drive the media and academia, and an inaccurately informed workforce reinforces that selfishness.

Anyone who has read The Federalist Papers knows that those who wrote the American Constitution had significant doubts about anybody with unbridled power. Their skepticism shows in the Constitution and has been a big part of its success for more than two centuries while other ambitious political experiments all around the world have failed.

The economic counterpart of constitutional checks and balances is an economy where everyone who wants to profit has to compete with everyone else, and everyone is allowed to participate in a portion of the value they help create, i.e., as stakeholders. Its results are not perfect, but it beats the next best thing by a high margin.

Unfortunately, many of the imperfections are caused by the lack of checks and balances in the media and academia.

One way to start resolving the imperfections is to educate our employees about the relationship of expenses to income. Then compare your profit to the returns available to your shareholders from alternative investment opportunities. The ultimate theme that must be reinforced is that *profit creates jobs*. It is profit that creates financial opportunity for all stakeholders, and if the profit we create is not adequate, the shareholders have every right, in fact an obligation, to invest their resources in something that will create jobs.

101

Figure 8-3 Explaining Profitability

Manufacturing

Payroll & Benefits 34%	Materials 30%	Marketing 10%	Plant 11%	Misc 3%	Profit 12%
Income					

Banking

Payroll & Benefits 23%	Interest 38%	Equipmt & Occup 8%	All Other 19%	Profit 12%
Interest Income 93%				Non-Int Income 7%

Typical Return from Shareholders' Alternative Investment Opportunities

Stock Market	9-24%
Bonds	4-9%
CDs	5%
Savings	3%

This simplistic format can be used to communicate to your employees the comparative expense(s) to profit. Be sure to revise it to demonstrate graphically the percent of each category and have "box" demonstrate that percentage of the total. Then discuss the implications of the shareholders' alternative investment opportunities.

Commitment to Coach

In studying the key principles of coaching to improve performance, Whitmore[2] concludes that expressions such as "our people are our greatest resource," "we must empower all our staff," "we must release latent potential," "downsizing," "developing responsibility," and "getting the most out of our people" have become cliches in recent years. Their true meaning remains as valid today as when they were first coined, but all too often they are hollow words. Coaching for performance is just what it says—a means of obtaining optimum performance—but one that demands fundamental changes in attitude, in managerial behavior, and in organizational structure. It gives the cliches substance.

All must commit to such change. However, there will be plenty of cynical responses:

> "We have made all these grand changes in the past and they did not make any difference."

> "No sooner will we have made this change than we will have to change again."

> "Let's do nothing, it's just another new flavor of the month."

These are the anxieties of many who are threatened by inevitable uncertainties, but the questions and concerns are also very valid and we need to address them if we are going to manage change well.

So the culture has to change—but from what to what? The answer depends more on perspective than on consensus, because any new culture will have to deliver higher levels of performance. No corporation is going to take the risks and undergo the upheavals involved in major change just for the sake of change, or just to be more generous to employees. Culture change will be, and needs to be, performance driven.

So what is the most important application of coaching?

Only when coaching principles govern or underlie all management behavior and interactions, as they certainly will in time, will the full force of people's performance potential be released.

On unlocking a person's potential

Socrates voiced the same thoughts some 2000 years ago, but somehow his philosophy was lost to material reductionism. The pendulum has swung back and coaching, if not Socrates, is here to stay. The emergence in psychological understanding is of a more optimistic model of humankind. The old behaviorist view was that we are little more than empty vessels into which everything has to be poured. The new model suggests that we are more like an acorn, which contains within it all the potential to be a magnificent oak tree. We need nourishment, encouragement, and light to reach toward, but the potential is already within.

The first key element to coaching is awareness, which is the product of focused attention, concentration, and clarity. It is the gathering and the clear perception of the relevant facts and information, and the ability to determine what is relevant. That ability will include an understanding of systems, dynamics, relationships between things and people, and inevitably some understanding of psychology.

Responsibility is the other key concept or goal of coaching. When we truly accept responsibility for our thoughts and our actions, our commitment to them rises and so does our performance. When we are ordered to be responsible, expected to be or even given responsibility, if we do not fully accept it performance does not rise. We may do the job because there is an implied threat if we do not, but doing something to avoid a threat does not optimize performance. To truly feel responsible invariably involves choice.

The struggle with time and commitment

Many managers too frequently find themselves firefighting, struggling to get the job done. By their own admission they are unable to devote the time they feel they should to long-term planning, to visioning, to taking the overview, to surveying alternatives, the competition, new products and the like. Most importantly, they are unable to devote the time to growing their people and to staff development. Rather they send them to a training course and frustrate themselves when they realize that that doesn't get the job done.

So how can managers find time to coach their staff? The paradoxical answer is that *if* they coach their staff, the developing staff shoulders much greater responsibility, freeing the manager from firefighting not only to coach more but to attend to those issues that only he or she can address. So growing people is enlightened self-interest to create added value.

A manager's task is simple—to get the job done and to grow his or her staff. If managers manage by the principles of coaching, they both get the job done to a higher quality and develop their people simultaneously.

Summary

In order to realize the power of people's performance potential, coaching principles must govern or serve as a foundation for all management behavior and interactions.

Coaching is unlocking a person's potential to maximize their own performance. It is helping people to learn rather than teaching them. The attraction of telling or dictating is that, besides being quick and easy, it provides the dictator with the feeling of being in control. This is, however, a fallacy. The dictator upsets and demotivates staff. Feedback is discouraged because people are not being heard. The result is that in the traditional environment the workforce is subservient in the traditional manager's presence. However, people behave differently, with resentment and with poor performance at best, when the manager's back is turned. Then the traditional manager is anything but in control.

The first key element to coaching is awareness and the second is responsibility or accountability. When all stakeholders accept accountability for their actions, management's commitment to support them rises and so does overall performance.

One of the many challenges in today's workplace is finding time to introduce new processes. But ultimately, the time invested yields more time for managers as their staff takes on more responsibility. So growing people is enlightenment to self-interest.

The teaching of the coaching process has become a new industry. A recommended reading list is provided in Appendix IV. The process is proven and documented and deserves the attention of all organizations with the commitment not only to survive and prosper, but to maximize their potential.

PART 3

"*STAKEHOLDERS*"
A Catalyst for Positive Change

CHAPTER 9

Alignment with Strategic Planning

*"If you know the enemy and know
yourself, you need not fear the results of
a hundred battles. If you know yourself
but not the enemy, for every victory
gained, you will also suffer a defeat. If
you do not know the enemy or yourself,
you will succumb in every battle."*
—SUN TZU (500 B.C.)

Strategically, the *"STAKEHOLDERS"* methodology is not applicable to every business environment. It is not applicable to business environments where:

1. Competition in the market place is in decline.

2. The workforce will not accept accountability.

3. The leadership is not committed to excellence.

4. Management cannot justify the time it takes to become higher performing because of lack of commitment to excellence.

5. Ownership does not require a high performing company.

All other work environments are applicable.

The only purpose for a strategic plan is to create a focus on how the organization will differentiate itself from its competition. If there is little or no competition, there is no need for strategic planning or for performance compensation. If there is competition and the number of competitors is increasing, the organization cannot survive without strategic planning. However, compensation strategies must be tied to the strategic priorities and the budgeting process. And, performance compensation must be defined in terms of strategic priorities rather than by expense control (budgeting).

In the more than 600 companies that I have worked with, I have never seen a management team's budget or performance compensation tied to strategic priorities at the outset. In each and every case, even in high-performing companies, the traditional budgeting process was driven by expense control and by manipulating the numbers to create an expected bottom-line goal. Budgeting is rarely coordinated with strategic priorities and is never aligned with the strategic prerequisite to maximize long-term shareholder value, i.e., to balance profit with growth, quality and productivity priorities.

When I first created the "STAKEHOLDERS" methodology in 1983, it was out of the frustration of recognizing that traditional compensation programs were no longer relevant because they were never tied to strategic priorities. Therefore performance compensation was never designed to maximize long-term shareholder value. As I assisted companies in facilitating their strategic planning sessions, I also began to realize that too often the strategic plans were placed on the shelf and left until the next strategic planning retreat. I thought if I could tie everyone's compensation to the strategic planning priorities, their people would be more dedicated to fulfilling their strategic planning commitments. My plan, then, was to facilitate the strategic planning process and tie compensation to strategic priorities to ensure that everyone internalized the action plans that they committed to.

The third influence was my observation that even good management teams think in terms of "what can we afford" when it comes to creating a strategic plan or designing a performance compensation program. They see performance compensation as an expense; therefore they want to budget for performance reward rather than thinking in terms of maximizing performance.

Of course, these observations came over a period of time and evolved in my mind's eye as I found people continually saying one thing about their strategic need to manage change and then conducting business as usual when they got back to their day-to-day responsibilities. Why is it that otherwise brilliant people who plan to do things one way end up conducting their activities in a completely different manner?

So my original aim was to ensure that companies followed the appropriate chronological process—create the strategic plan, then action plans, budget for the action plans and strategic priorities, and then create a performance compensation program to stimulate everyone in the organization to focus on the strategic objectives.

Interestingly enough, as correct as the process may have seemed at the time, I had designed it entirely backwards. I was caught up in my own strategic thinking paradigm as I attempted to break away from old ones And I was wrong!

I was wrong because the budgeting process still drove the strategic planning priorities and the performance compensation system.

The appropriate chronology is to first think about what the organization can become if it could maximize its potential over the next three-to-five years. The first step, then, is to create a three-to-five-year performance model balancing profit with growth, quality and productivity. Once the five-year model is created, it becomes much easier for each member of the management team to think: "What do we need to concentrate on in the next year in order to stay on track for the now-established long-term strategic priorities to balance profit, growth, quality and productivity?" From that discussion and exercise, a one-year performance model is built. The one-year performance model creates a matrix with a minimum level of expectation to balance profit, growth, quality and productivity. Then, the stretch goals to maximize performance for the coming year are agreed upon.

At this juncture, the management team has established a mindset based on maximizing potential. Now they have the appropriate mindset to define the strategic priorities to maximize potential over the short-term (one year) and the long-term (three-to-five years).

The second step is to facilitate the strategic planning process that will establish strategic priorities and tactical action plans and align them with the goal levels that have been identified in the one-year and five-year performance models.

The primary purpose of the strategic planning process should be reinforced by a prerequisite ground rule: Accuracy is defined by focus. Accuracy must come first, and momentum should follow accuracy. Focus is the ability to achieve a targeted, predetermined set of priority objectives that directly impact effectiveness in reviewing, refining, adjusting and adapting to strategic accuracy. Once accuracy—in other words, agreed-upon focus—is determined, momentum can then be instilled.

Momentum is the ability to control the level of success within a targeted timeframe. Momentum deals with consistency in the process. Consistent intensity drives a group's ability to be successful. The planning process must be as concise, simple and uncomplicated as possible. The objective of the planning process is to *implement* successfully, *not* to develop a plan. The objective is to create a blueprint as a resource to ensure success and support— to align the strategic priorities to the performance model. Success, then, is the product of implementation.

Strategic planning recognizes that we must do things differently in the future as we evolve in an ever-changing and competitive environment. Commitment to success demands an investment in time and dedicated effort so that accuracy is first achieved and then reinforced through successful implementation. Consistency is essential. Shortcuts result in mediocrity.

Strategic planning is the product of strategic thinking. It is a concentrated vision of the future. It defines where we are going and how we are going to get there. It should be creative, insightful, clever, bold and it should expand dramatically beyond what is currently being done. It should include previously unexamined options, possibilities and alternatives.

Vision is a prerequisite for a successful strategic program. Therefore, creating the "*STAKEHOLDERS*" strategic model and then abstracting it into a one-year tactical performance model is a prerequisite so that all participants have a consistent reference to implement successfully.

The strategic focus and issues must be communicated and clearly understood by all of those involved in implementing the plan. The entire staff must understand and become a part of achieving the organization's priorities. The staff must become enthusiastic about the vision and commit to the mission and its objectives concerning the organization's position in the marketplace, prioritized market segments, and other factors entailed in implementation. Everyone must have a thorough understanding of their role and accept their role in corporate, team and individual goal achievement. The effort begins with improved communication. The catalyst for improved communication will be the "STAKEHOLDERS" methodology. The result will be clear understanding and an enthusiastic endorsement by all who are involved.

The Benefits Of Strategic Planning

Those who understand the importance of and who therefore support the strategic planning process recognize that all organizations, no matter how large or small, have limited resources. Strategic planning followed by successful implementation ensures that limited financial, physical, and personnel resources are invested in the strategic priorities and action plans that will maximize the organization's potential. Planning also improves internal communications because it defines explicit responsibilities and fosters accountability. Effective planning and successful implementation help coordinate both management and staff in working toward the organization's primary purpose and priorities.

In most organizations, people are doing many things right. However, too often, they are not concentrating on doing the right things. Strategic planning directs everyone to concentrate on doing the right things right, the most important things first, in order to achieve strategic and tactical priorities.

The most critical step toward ensuring that strategic priorities are always incorporated in decision-making is to tie the achievement of strategic priorities to performance compensation.

Today, successful planning is a concise, intuitive process that consists of reinforcing a corporate mission with objectives that are based on an assessment of the competitive environment. An op-

113

erational plan of action is created that has explicit implementation schedules and responsibility assignments. This provides the follow-up and review tools critical to successful implementation. The key to successful planning is the process, which includes structured follow-up on never-ending implementation activities.

Resistance To The Planning Process

By nature, the strategic planning process is very comprehensive. However, it need not be complicated or complex. Nonetheless, while many management teams have initiated elements of the planning process, few have made a total commitment to implement the strategic plan. Resistance to and the lack of commitment to strategic planning is the product of seven unacceptable mindsets.

1. *Compensation.* "Performance compensation is never really tied to strategic (long-term) goals."

2. *Skill.* "I do not know or my management team does not know enough about strategic planning to be effective."

3. *Unknown Future.* "No one can forecast the future. Things are changing too fast for us to waste time planning for the unknown."

4. *Security.* "I don't want my staff or my board to really understand what I am trying to do." Or, "I am trying to position to sell my company in the next three years, and I cannot afford to allow that to be known."

5. *Don't Fix It.* "We've been successful before without planning. There is no need to fix what isn't broken."

6. *Time.* "There isn't enough time for me and my officers to serve our customers and set time aside for planning meetings."

7. *Expense.* "Strategic planning is too costly and a wasteful effort. The plans always end up on the shelf anyway."

Let's look at each of these seven excuses:

1. Compensation. Compensation can be and must be tied to achievement of strategic priorities.

2. Skill. Strategic planning skills are mastered the minute a participant recognizes that planning is an on-going process. Successful planning, like a business, should begin small and continually evolve into bigger and better things. To ensure that strategic planning becomes a process, a systematic approach must be developed that enables management to separate the process into manageable phases with objectives that can be achieved within a reasonable timeframe.

Learning how to incorporate the more-comprehensive and complex planning skills is part of the process. The techniques used initially are much less sophisticated. As time passes, each participant improves in his or her skill, knowledge, awareness, and, finally, support for the strategic planning process.

3. *Unknown Future.* Strategic planning has nothing to do with defining the future. Decisions exist only in the present. The critical decision-making process deals with defining what needs to be done today to be ready for an uncertain tomorrow. As the senior management team becomes more skilled in planning, the participants begin to realize how futile it is to try to project the future.

An uncertain future is no excuse not to plan; rather, it argues for the need to plan. Initially, one of the great benefits of strategic planning is the improved communication created throughout the management team. For the first time, key players begin to understand how each other thinks, and they start to perceive priorities and the need for better coordination among their individual responsibilities. Eventually, that advantage of understanding permeates the entire organization.

Comparisons of activity against projected priorities also enable the management team to modify future plans and add perspective to the planning process. And management's accountability for making plans happen—that is, for implementation—becomes the most important next step in improving the planning process.

Finally, an uncertain future is the justification for the element of planning called contingency planning. Contingency planning is nothing more than an organized, pre-arranged method of changing the direction of a business in the event it exceeds or does not achieve desired goals. The strategic planning process provides a tool for interpreting uncertainty and directing corrective action.

4. Security. A reluctance to inform officers and staff about an intent to sell a business very often is an expression of a deep-seated apprehension about individual management skills. In weighing whether to inform the staff of ownership's intent, vision, strategy, and driving force, it is important to understand that:

- A staff will both interpret and misinterpret management's failure to communicate. Also, the failure to communicate seriously strains management's credibility and will result in reduced productivity.
- Management must depend on the staff to maximize the organization's potential. Anything less than keeping people fully informed results in the organization failing to realize the opportunities presented.
- The plan should be communicated so that the organization functions as a cohesive unit working together toward the same goals. Equally important, communication ensures that the organization does not work counterproductively.
- Both management and staff have much at stake—income, pension plans, favorable working conditions and future careers full of opportunity. It is not only fair, it is ethical to keep the various options above board.

The latter point is very important. If, in fact, the decision is to position the company to sell, or position it to sell as a contingency, then the options acceptable to management should be communicated. Otherwise, the rationale comes full circle; in which case, see the first bullet point above. Instead, the way to counter the disadvantages of communicating these strategic priorities (to sell) is to create the appropriate performance compensation system.

5. Don't Fix It. Although some organizations have been successful in the past without comprehensive strategic planning, few will survive in the future without it.

Another, more obvious, reason to begin strategic planning, even if prior success has been experienced without it, is that all companies and organizations are facing ever-changing environments. What worked in the past to promote growth or any other achievable goal has nothing to do with what will work in the future. The automobile, healthcare, finance, steel, and airline industries are all proven examples. It is not prudent to rely on past success to predict future success. Conditions change, and therefore management must change if it is to compete successfully in a more competitive marketplace.

6. Time. Strategic planning does take time. However, contemporary strategic planning techniques have reduced the time requirement significantly. Technologically utilizing the "*STAKE-HOLDER*" models in preparation for strategic planning will further expedite the process.

7. Expense. A contemporary management team can ill-afford not to plan effectively. The very essence of management is to maximize potential, which requires planning. A successful planning process eliminates low-priority activity and directs all resources toward the activities having the greatest priority.

Action Planning

Action planning must be directed exclusively at the strategic and tactical priorities that are prerequisite to supporting the quantitative strategic priorities of the three-to-five-year and the one-year "*STAKEHOLDERS*" performance models.

Action planning is, in fact, an effort whereby the organization develops priorities and responds with specific activities to resolve its weaknesses and market limitations while building on its strengths as they apply to market opportunities. Action planning must:

- Stress the positive relative to opportunities and strengths.
- Shore up only those weaknesses that have direct impact on the ability to maximize potential.

Action planning must focus the attack on the organization's primary competitors' vulnerabilities as defined by the discussion of the organization's competitive advantage.

Strategic action planning tells management, supervisors, and staff which ropes to climb and which ropes to skip.

The action planning procedure is most effective when the group can be broken up into work groups. The participants should have special expertise or interest in the area to be action planned.

Once the strategic planning and action planning processes are completed, the management team must review the three to five-year strategic "STAKEHOLDERS" model and the one-year tactical model. This review is to ensure that the strategic priorities established in the strategic plan and the subsequent action planning will support the achievement of Columns 3 to 5 in the tactical model and maximize potential in the strategic five-year model.

Budget Alignment

Once the strategic planning priorities are aligned to the "STAKEHOLDERS" model, the budgeting process can begin. The process is simple and accurate, which is not typical of traditional budgeting processes.

Because the baselines of all the subordinate models reconcile with the baselines of the corporate model, the expense values in the productivity ratio of the subordinate models drive the budgeting process for each subordinate unit as well as the corporate business unit.

For example, if the "STAKEHOLDERS" performance model is driven off of last year actual values, the baseline overhead or expense value or the overhead value in the productivity ratio will equal last year expenses. If baseline is a value other than last year actual, such as ROE, ROA, ROI, or a pre-tax income value, then the productivity expense value is calculated based on existing growth KPIs times an acceptable margin level, minus the predetermined pre-tax income value. After the stretch values are agreed upon for each KPI, Column 1 or 2 or sometimes even Column 3 in the "STAKEHOLDERS" model is budget. By defining one of the specific columns in the model as budget, the overhead or expense value in the productivity ratio for that particular column has been established as budget for the coming year. Because all of the subordinate models reconcile with the senior model, the overall expense value for each one of the subordinate models will equal the overhead or expense value stated in the productivity ratio for that particular column. Therefore, if Column 2 is designated "budget" for the corporate model, Column 2 expense value under productivity will be budget for all subordinate models.

Reconfirming the budgeting process begins with the projections of additional expense to support the action plans for the subordinate models. During the construction of each subordinate model, the relative additional expense requirement for achieving each column level of performance is identified by the expense value in the productivity KPI.

Now the "budgeting process" is driven by action plans to maximize performance rather than by expense control to pacify board members and owners.

Summary

Strategic planning is back with a vengeance, but it is also back with a difference. Gone are the abstractions, sterility, and top-down arrogance.

Strategic planning has been streamlined, driven by strategic priorities and performance compensation to focus everyone on maximizing potential. The process has also been democratized by handing strategic planning over to teams of line and staff managers from different disciplines so they can create action plans to maximize their business unit's performance model. To keep the planning process as close to the realities of markets as possible, today's strategists say it should also include interaction with key customers and suppliers. This overall openness alone marks the revolution in strategic planning.

CHAPTER 10

A Vehicle for
Positive Cultural Change

*"The preparation for total war
must begin before the outbreak of
overt hostilities."*
—ERICH LUDENDORFF

Corporate culture represents the sum of beliefs, standards, values, attitudes, and behavior patterns that are shared and adhered to within an organization. As might be expected, the weaker the overall culture, the greater the likelihood there will be strong and potentially conflicting subcultures, each with its own set of values and priorities.

Corporate culture is more than something an organization just has, because culture can produce a profound impact on the daily behavior of all organizational members. In a very real sense, culture defines what the organization is! A high performing organization will be characterized by strong, positive, performance-oriented culture, while culture in poorly performing companies will tend to be weak and fragmented, with little or no emphasis on performance-oriented values.

Leadership and Cultural Change

Cultural change begins when someone with sufficient power and influence recognizes that the prevailing "how we do things around here" no longer supports strategic initiatives necessary for superior performance.

An organization's culture can be its single greatest attribute when the culture is strong, positive, strategically supportive, and in tune with the demands imposed by economic and competitive realities. Because the process of crafting and implementing a high-performance corporate culture will invariably require some degree of culture modification, it is important that the organization's leaders understand what to expect when the process of cultural change is undertaken.

Bear in mind that change, such as that which must take place to implement *"STAKEHOLDERS,"* leads to a dynamic shift in corporate culture. Existing culture has been developed over time based on what "has been acceptable" and, therefore, there will be resistance to change. For example, the dynamic shift in an environment driven by *"STAKEHOLDERS"* will be a shift to high performance through accountability.

What must be communicated with great clarity is that this change, this shift in corporate culture, is the result of the realization that the organization has not yet learned how to maximize its potential, to maximize everyone's potential, and that this change is to get the organization on the path to doing exactly that.

What would cause a person or group to be willing to depart from the present state for a transition state of ambiguity or insecurity?

Significant change in any environment will be sustained *only* if those affected learn to understand that the present way of doing things yields less to both the organization and the individual. Stated in more day-to-day, practical terms, "No one will change until they understand that the pain for not changing is greater than the pain of change." Therefore, positive reinforcement in the form of structured counseling is often needed for those dealing with management change in a business environment. That is why the "Coaching *STAKEHOLDERS*" sessions are prerequisite for success.

Internal management strategies must be created for all organizations in transition. Change demands new management skills and new leadership skills in order to maximize the great potential of each team participant, which is the essence of a more-competitive corporate culture.

What is a Corporate Culture?

Corporate culture is the learned pattern of thought and behavior of an organization. It is the way an organization has agreed to do things. In successful organizations, there is a corporate culture, an observable pattern of behavior, from the boardroom to the supply room.

Coining slogans and making statements about instilling a positive corporate culture does not create a positive corporate culture. It cannot just sound good; there must be belief. Management must constantly demonstrate its commitment. For example, in reinforcing its commitment to "*STAKEHOLDERS*," management must repeatedly demonstrate its commitment to accountability for high performance, and that mediocrity will not be tolerated. Then, and only then, a successful culture of accountability spreads throughout the organization as a corporate value.

Creating the Environment for Self Motivation

How are people motivated to achieve high performance? People do things for one of two reasons. They do good work because they want to, or they work because they have to. When employees want to do good work, they are much more likely to excel.

This basic concept is an expansion of Maslow's hierarchy of needs. The importance of reviewing Maslow's pyramid is reinforced by the recognition that the very foundation of everyone's needs is the basic physiological need to survive. Once a person's fear of failure is resolved, all motivation to prohibit failure ends. Traditional reward programs reward for improved performance, but have no mechanism to penalize deterioration of one or more performance measures. "*STAKEHOLDERS*" resolves that void by requiring a balance of performance measures with a penalty to the reward pool for deterioration of any key performance indicator. Then, and only then, people will motivate themselves to prevent any one performance indicator from deteriorating.

Figure 10-1 Maslow's Hierarchy of Needs

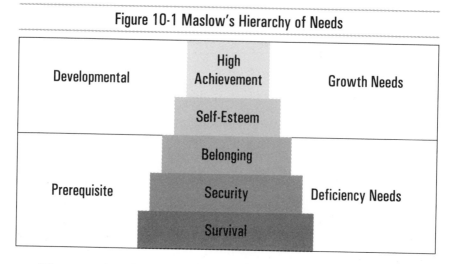

The next level of need is the need for security. The fear of being fired or the fear of being dealt with in an arbitrary fashion are threats to security. The threat of firing employees will motivate them to act, but it will only motivate them to do just enough not to get fired. This is the basic reason why most individual performance review programs are less than successful.

The third level is the need for belonging, that is, the need to be affiliated and accepted by other people. When a person is not accepted by other people, it triggers the fear of rejection. The fear of rejection, again, is a motivator. Employees can be scolded, shouted at, chastised, or approval withheld, but the only result will be that they will do exactly what they need to do in order to avoid the negative experience, and no more.

Even higher in the pyramid of needs is the desire for esteem or recognition. People have to feel great about themselves and be praised and recognized by others for their performance. One of the two biggest irritants and demoralizers in all of business is that management does not recognize an employee for a job well done. There is nothing more demoralizing to a person than to do a job as well as he or she possibly can and have the effort completely ignored by management. In effect, management is saying that no matter how well you do the job, it really does not matter.

If good performance is not recognized, how motivated will a person be to work smarter next time? Most managers do not realize that their people are dying for recognition. We all are! Most employees are dying to give their whole heart to their work; they want to make a contribution. Companies that recognize their employees, praise them, and give them continuous feedback and approval have created the corporate culture to succeed.

Finally, the very highest need is the need to achieve and fulfill potential. If management can create a corporate environment in which employees have the opportunity to fulfill their potential, to become everything they are capable of becoming, and to achieve all the success they can achieve, they will make a commitment and will throw their whole heart and soul into their work responsibilities.

The survival need, the security need, and the belonging need are all *deficiency* needs. Deficiency needs are such that once they are satisfied, motivation to perform is no longer present. The higher-level needs—the need for self-esteem and the need to achieve—are *growth* needs. If management can get their employees plugged into their growth needs, it will find that they become excited about fulfilling themselves and achieving everything they are capable of achieving.

Growth needs act as a perpetual motivator. A week or a month or a year later, employees will still be motivated to do the very best they can. "*STAKEHOLDERS*" is a catalyst to fulfill growth needs. In contrast, if management motivates with deficiency needs, fear of failure, fear of rejection, withdrawal of approval, or dismissal threats, the motivation will work only as long as management keeps up the threats.

Motivation

Management has long been preoccupied with developing the ability to motivate people, to find what it takes to arouse employees to quality performance, and to assume the responsibility for cultural behaviors. In this pursuit they take courses and attend seminars in order to acquire the dynamic qualities of elite motivational speakers, and they adopt their theories with hope that those tactics will empower them with such abilities.

The assumption here is that motivation, an internal desire to take action, can be influenced or imposed from external sources, i.e., from motivational speakers, motivational practices, and motivational personalities. This is a semantic misinterpretation, however. What we have traditionally called motivation has been wrongly aligned with the qualities of inspiration. Inspiration—derived from external emotional triggers such as enthusiasm, excitement, encouragement—often arouses an individual into action, but it may or may not result in long-term behavior modification. Once the emotional stimulus is no longer externally imposed, action wanes.

Motivation, in the professional realm, may be externally triggered only when an individual's pre-existing, internal values are met with one or more of the *growth needs*. These include the opportunity to contribute; to acquire new responsibilities; to grow socially, spiritually, or financially; to be recognized for one's efforts; to prove one's self-worth; to acquire job security, or others.

Only at the merging of pre-existing, internal values with external growth opportunity comes long-term, and self-imposed, behavior modification.

Consider this. As leaders and managers, do we actually motivate employees directly or do we create an environment—a culture—in which their values can be realized? Are we most immediately responsible for an employee's level of enthusiasm or for the potential to develop an enthusiastic environment?

Perhaps we must acknowledge our managerial limitations. Can we actually be responsible for changing someone's psychological perception and behaviors or do we simply have the opportunity to allow (or deny) the ideal psychology and perceptions that foster growth?

Certainly this is not to say that managers should be anything less than encouraging, enthusiastic, excited, and anxious, but that it is important to understand from where long-term behavior modification comes. Encouragement and enthusiasm contribute to the daily maintenance of a positive work atmosphere and can provide an inspirational example, but alone they cannot accomplish long-term performance modification.

Long-term behavior modification for increased performance, relative to motivation, is the result of offering the ideal circumstances in which stakeholders feel they can fully pursue their values and maximize their potential. Recognizing the need to provide the opportunity for people to fulfill their goals and expectations for themselves and their team is at the root of understanding motivation. When we arrive at this perspective, we understand the *prerequisite to create a work environment where people can motivate themselves to excel.*

Negative reinforcement is a full-time job, and no one can afford the effort or the results. The minute a manager's back is turned, people stop performing. Therefore, the key to successful leadership is to move as many people up the pyramid of needs as rapidly as possible by removing barriers to self-motivation while increasing reward. This is leadership; the skill to elicit extraordinary performance from ordinary people.

The University of Nebraska football program is a good example of the importance to create an environment where people will motivate themselves to excel. The University is very unusual among most Division 1-A football programs in that it has such a small population base. And weather is never good at the height of the recruiting season. Needless to say, the University's recruiting classes have never been ranked among the top 10 and rarely among the top 20 classes nationally. If you look at the record, however, Nebraska has ranked among the top 25 teams in the nation for 31 consecutive years, 22 times ranked in the top 10 and 5 National Championships. If there is any validity to the rankings of the recruiting gurus, the NU staff has been able to maximize the talents of players to an unusual degree. However, it takes leadership to build a winning team.

Building a Winning Team

Building a winning team consists of six prerequisite steps:

Step 1 is *personnel development*. Eliminate annual reviews. Annual reviews have proven to be a negative exercise and therefore are ill-fated, disliked, and a waste of time. Annual reviews are dreaded because they serve little purpose, and often are feared because they are so subjective. They are driven by myopic thinking because the people conducting the exercise are (typically) poorly trained. Therefore, annual reviews do not provide a positive or constructive contribution to the work environment.

Contemporary business environments have eliminated the traditional annual review in favor of a very positive and stimulating exercise that has been appropriately designated as a *Personal Development Assessment* (PDA). PDA is a process that should be performed at least quarterly because it is a very constructive experience for everyone involved (See Appendix V.)

The PDA is a vital tool to help an organization improve its overall level of performance. The process recognizes and takes advantage of the fact that the contribution of each and every individual has a tremendous impact on how successful the company is as a whole. As such, the PDA has been developed to help identify individual strengths and weaknesses. With this information, leadership can create an environment where individual strengths are recognized and utilized. At the same time, individual weaknesses can be turned into improvement opportunities.

Step 2 is *purpose*. What is the purpose of the company? What is its mission? What are its basic values? People need purpose. The company has to stand for something greater than simply making money!

The most inspiring external purpose is serving other people by doing something important. That is what keeps people motivated. That is what keeps people working exhaustively during crisis in hospitals and that is what keeps people working with such focus in response to accidents or disasters.

Step 3 is *excellence*. Striving toward excellence is one of the most influential, perpetual motivators. Excellence equals motivation because excellence is a journey, not a destination. Excellence in an organization is never achieved; it is always aspired to. When everybody in a company is striving to do things in an excellent fashion and is succeeding, even if only on occasion, everyone in the company feels very good about continuing to contribute. Everyone wants to be on a winning team, and winning in business becomes equally important. This is why an environment must be created and reinforced in which people are asked to participate only in activities that they know they can be successful at. First, ask employees to do only those things they know how to do well. Then, after they experience doing something well, they can be asked to extend themselves; they will have become enthusiastic about their ability to contribute by being successful.

Step 4 is *building a consensus.* Getting people to become involved in the decision-making process is critically important. There is a one-to-one relationship between the degree of consensus in a decision and the degree of commitment. That is not to say that there has to be universal agreement on every decision. Sometimes consensus can emerge just from people understanding why decisions were made. Whether doing long-range planning, preparing budgets, or forecasting sales, it is very important to get people together and ask them how they feel about it. Decisions handed down from above do not produce. In contrast, when people are involved in the decision, they will work very hard to achieve its goals and to achieve them within the timeframe and the budget agreed upon.

Step 5 is *team-building.* Traditional thinking calls for management to assume a role in which it is a stern taskmaster, to stay aloof and keep a distance from the staff. Although this thinking is still being taught today, it has no place in a competitive environment. Successful organizations no longer work out of the traditional pyramid. Today, in order to maximize everyone's contribution, companies function so that decision-making is the focal point around which everything else revolves. The result is a centrally focused organization of coordinated functions, thus maximizing the potential of the company's limited financial, physical, technological, and personnel resources.

Step 6 is *reward.* Rewards to include recognition and value must be linked to team performance first and then to individual contribution. If an organization has a history of promoting or compensating employees on the basis of seniority rather than on the basis of performance, management *must* undo these inequities before it can prepare the organization to compete successfully. High achievers and highly productive people will demand an environment with performance specifications.

Who stays in an environment in which people are compensated for tenure? People who do not perform. Who stays in an environment in which people are compensated for performance? High performers!!

Therefore, the best way to begin to create a successful performance compensation system is to establish a corporate goal to work toward 30% to 50% of total compensation based on performance.

Self-Concept = Performance

There is a direct relationship between self-concept and performance. Self-concept regulates everything we do, and, interestingly, we can *never* perform beyond the level at which we are convinced that we can perform. What that really says is that people will never perform beyond their level of self-concept.

There have been extensive studies proving that people perform within the parameters that they set for themselves. If management wants more, it must plan and set goals with employees that they can achieve—first, in their minds, next in reality. This concept is not the same as the power of positive thinking. This is belief!

A successful, positive corporate culture can create a self-concept that results in success throughout the entire organization. The vast majority of your people have the capacity to get the job done.

Performance is always governed by self-concept. Self-concept has little to do with reality. Self-concept has to do with perception. If people think they will be effective, they will be effective. Conversely, if people are led to be or allowed to be ineffective, they will be ineffective. As in the old adage, *"If at first you believe you won't succeed, sky diving is not for you."*

Successful leaders give employees the confidence to believe in what they can do. They do not force employees beyond their level of self-confidence. Most important of all, people need winning experiences. The only thing management should insist upon is that their employees continue to improve their self-concept of what they want to do and then work to reach the next step beyond their present level of performance. Employees will do that because they know they can never be unsuccessful doing what they know they can do.

Commitment to a Successful Culture

The #1 and most important prerequisite for success is management's commitment. Much attention has been given to the need to create a successful culture, but little is understood about what that commitment from management really means.

By definition, corporate culture is a commitment to a belief that exerts a powerful influence over the entire workforce. People stimulate cultures. Therefore, successful managers manage and shape their corporate cultures in ways that are most desirable for their particular organizations.

It is necessary to build a spirit and a belief that will result in a set of values, standards and customs that can be ascribed to by all personnel. A company must have corporate values to assure dignity and opportunity for each employee, which, in turn, ensures that each employee's identity is fused with that of the corporation.

A successful organization has a network that keeps a culture alive by its belief in the company and the organization's purpose. A successful culture provides for a strong personal identity as well as a clear understanding of what the organization stands for.

The key point in developing a successful culture is to manage people in such a way that they become a part of the organization.

What are the attributes of a successful culture? First, everyone works hard in promoting the culture. Everyone understands the implications and believes in the very purpose of the organization. All participants, either consciously or intuitively, reinforce a loyalty and cohesiveness throughout the organization. Successful companies are those that pay close attention to cohesiveness.

Values, standards and expectations are the core of the culture. Values are crystallized by setting goals and establishing a system for measuring and rewarding goal achievement.

Coining slogans or making idle statements about instilling a positive culture will not create a positive culture. It cannot just sound good. There must be a dedication on the part of all stakeholders.

Values and standards must filter down from the executive suite. All stakeholders will choose from only those values that are consistently emphasized. It is not a matter of pronouncing what the values are. Values are created and reinforced by watching what the company actually does. Actions communicate the belief and the commitment. Stakeholders do not listen to what is said, they "listen" to what is done.

The culture of accountability must be articulated as a commitment and be represented by example. Only then will the staff understand that high performance through excellence is the very purpose of the organization.

Summary

The transition will not always be an easy one. People get attached to their previous cultures, their previous values, standards and ceremonies.

A change in culture usually is opposed by most employees unless they recognize that the change provides intrinsic benefit to each participant. Attention must be paid to the transition as cultures are reshaped. It must also be recognized and appreciated that many people perceive they may be losing something they want to hold on to.

There also must be a consensus before change can succeed. And there needs to be a process that will help the organization understand that consensus. Culture is the major barrier to change because it influences the lives of all stakeholders.

Introducing a positive culture of high performance and accountability will require an investment in personnel training and systems that was previously unnecessary. Therefore, the investment in creating a high-performance culture will require special attention to maximizing efficiencies in management systems and productivity from personnel.

Efficient management systems can be acquired. Productive people, however, will seek those organizations that recognize and value high productivity. If management accepts mediocrity in any area of the organization—particularly among its personnel—it not only will discourage highly motivated and productive people from joining the organization, it will be unable to retain those that it does hire.

A productive environment stimulates productive people. Conversely, acceptance of mediocrity in any area of an organization discourages productivity throughout the entire organization. Consistency is important. Good people just won't stay in a mediocre environment.

Equally important, management's acceptance of mediocrity is an insult to those people who are productive. The inferred message is that productive efforts are unnecessary, unrecognized and without merit. Productivity begets productivity. Tolerating mediocrity encourages mediocrity. And a mediocre organization cannot compete in today's business environment.

Successful leadership strategies may be something entirely foreign to some managers. However, with the proper perspective and provided with the necessary tools, managers and supervisors can take comfort in knowing that maximizing potential in their area of responsibility is close at hand. The potential is always there. It only requires commitment to understanding what it takes to make it happen and that commitment begins with incorporating the six steps to building a winning team. Once commitment has been made, managing change is a prerequisite, the subject of the next chapter.

CHAPTER 11

Managing Change

> *"There is nothing more difficult to
> take in hand, more perilous to conduct,
> or more uncertain in its outcome, than to
> take the lead in introducing a new order
> of things. Because the innovator has for
> enemies all those who have done well
> under the old conditions, and lukewarm
> defenders in those who may do well
> under the new."*
>
> —MACHIAVELLI

Change is inherent in all business environments. In response to market demands to create competitive advantage, management teams purchase new systems and introduce new disciplines. Over the years various management programs have been implemented in untold numbers of organizations. But research confirms that all too many experience an unacceptable level of success.

Perhaps a priority for the new program has not been demonstrated by the CEO and some managers have been preoccupied by short-term challenges. Or, it could be that most have not understood the need for, and therefore have not incorporated, all of the mechanisms, monitoring processes, or systems to support the necessary. In any event, it is clear that mere rhetoric will not make the necessary changes happen. Only commitment and action initiated by the CEO and the leadership team will cause the needed changes to occur.

Developing and/or maintaining a competitive company demands an enthusiastic transfer of CEO belief. That belief can be seen and felt throughout the organization. This means that the successful senior management team must not merely be able to implement decisions so that the organization maximizes its potential. They must become effective leaders of change.

Effective leaders of change understand that change in a business environment is very difficult for many people—parallel to personal experiences such as a divorce, or losing a loved one. Just as counseling is needed for personal change, professional counseling is often needed for those dealing with managing change in a business environment. Leadership must also understand the necessity to deal with change as an opportunity rather than as a danger.

Effective leaders of change must:

1. Recognize a certain amount of discomfort within the organization that will develop as a result of implementing "*STAKEHOLDERS*." Therefore, they hold workshops to discuss and resolve areas of discomfort.

2. Understand and recognize how to remedy this discomfort. Therefore, they must point out the positive benefits of participating.

3. Continually reinforce, support, and recognize those individuals who are most effected by change or who have been most resistant to change.

4. Address the unique barriers that exist within the organization that may jeopardize the success of "*STAKEHOLDERS*."

Each stakeholder will fall into one of three categories regarding change.

1. *Resist change*—feel safe under present conditions, comfort in the known, or fear that change will force them to work harder.

2. *Neutral*—curious of change but may be skeptical as to whether change will be beneficial to them.

3. *Support change*—in want of continual progress and achievement and enjoy change for the sake of change.

Figure 11-1

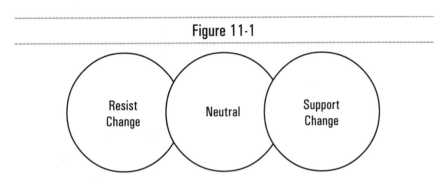

Successful Change, Defined

A good definition of successful change management is "that participants implement priority action plans and achieve objectives within a scheduled time and agreed upon budget."[1] There are five prerequisites to achieving major organizational change:

1. All participants need to understand the implications of the dangers and opportunities that exist within a timeframe that will allow appropriate action to be taken.

2. Participants, as well as the individual in charge of implementing change, need to understand the tremendous amount of discomfort that may develop as a result of change.

3. Participants must understand how to recognize and remedy the discomfort.

4. Management must continually reinforce, support, and recognize those individuals that are most affected by change.

5. The implementation team should address openly the unique barriers that exist within the organization that might jeopardize the desired results or goals.

Change is a Process

In approaching most projects, a critical mistake leaders often make is to assume change is an event, not a process. The successful leader of change must demonstrate an understanding that change is a process that must be carefully orchestrated at each level of the organization. To achieve movement from the "present state" to the "desired state," targets of change must pass through a "transition state," a period of high insecurity and ambiguity in which people are unfrozen from their current ways of doing things. For example, traditional methods of compensation based on tenure or subjective annual review contrast significantly with a *"STAKEHOLDERS"* environment where compensation is based on performance.

But what would cause a person or group to be willing to depart from the present state for a transitional state of ambiguity and insecurity? Only "pain" will provide the kind of motivation necessary. Substantial change, especially cultural change, must be more than merely "intellectually stimulating" before people will embrace it fully. A significant change will be sustained *only* if it is proven to those affected that the present way of doing things is more expensive than the price for transition. The pain of the status quo is the prime impetus for movement into the future.

There are two kinds of pain powerful enough to motivate change: current pain and anticipated pain. Current pain is generated by problems. Anticipated pain is caused by the possibility of missed opportunities or potential vulnerability. Current pain is seen when the leader says, "If we don't improve the performance of our operating unit immediately, management will either eliminate our division or they will reduce its size substantially." This leader is facing current problems and is missing current and future opportunities. A manager who anticipates the future is one who is in pain because the present definition of success will not sustain the organization in the future and he knows it.

Often, only the senior executives in an organization are in a position to know the problems their company may face months or years ahead. These managers must generate pain through the use of education and consequence management. This kind of pain will motivate the kinds of behavior needed to ensure future success. But whether the situation is one of current or anticipated pain, leaders must be aware that the critical task is to generate sufficient pain to motivate change without creating so much pain that yet more problems result. This balancing act is a key skill that leaders must demonstrate to successfully implement change in their organizations.

For many people the concept that only pain will motivate change is a hard one to accept or understand. However, a true, life-threatening incident will illustrate this key concept.

The survivor of a disastrous fire on an offshore drilling platform in the North Sea was being interviewed by Ted Koppel on *Nightline*. In matter-of-fact terms, the man described being awakened in the middle of the night by the explosion and alarms, of running to the edge of the platform, of jumping into the sea below, and of his subsequent rescue.

Mr. Koppel knew, however, that there was more to this story than the man's simple re-telling revealed, so he said, "Now, wait a minute. Let me get this straight. There was all manner of debris floating in the water. The water itself was covered with oil and on fire. And yet you awoke from a sound sleep, ran immediately to the edge of the platform, and without hesitation jumped fifteen stories into the water without knowing if you would survive the jump or if you would be rescued if you did survive the jump." Mr. Koppel paused for dramatic effect before asking, "Why in the world would you do that?"

The platform worker did not hesitate even a second: "Because if I did not jump, I was going to fry."

The platform worker undoubtedly knew the risks of making his jump. He knew that death was a possibility. He could also see explosions and roaring flames all around him. When it became clear to him that the possibility of survival B however remote B was better than the certainty of death, he made the jump.

The point is clear: a major, potentially cataclysmic change will not occur without pain as a motivator.

Practically speaking, *leadership is really a function of helping key persons in an organization understand the true costs of not changing.* Some of these costs include:

- The problem is not resolved.
- An opportunity is not exploited.
- Time, money, and people resources are wasted.
- Morale suffers.
- Job security for those involved is threatened.
- The department or company will cease to exist.

There are three other very important consequences if the leadership team is unable to fully implement needed changes. If left unattended, these consequences can become devastating to the long-term health of any organization. These consequences are:

- People within the organization will learn to ignore strategic directives.
- The organization loses confidence in the leadership because the leadership does not appear to be in control.
- Short-term comfort from status quo is replaced by an inability to survive.

Communicating the high costs of mismanaged change is the key to releasing people from the present state and moving them toward the desired state. But just broadcasting the costs of mismanaged change via various "pain messages" is not enough. They must go to the right people. Effective leaders of change have a clear understanding of the key roles and relationships involved in a change project, and they use this understanding to drive change throughout the organization.

Managing Change Requires Culture Change

The kind of change that a company must undergo to become a competitive institution in the 21st century is not merely a small, tactical adjustment. It will require a complete shift in culture, because whenever there is a discrepancy between culture and change, culture always wins. This kind of change cannot, of course, be implemented overnight, because a culture shift is a re-definition of what an organization is and how it defines success. The problem is compounded by the fact that even though culture is a very powerful force in a company's day-to-day operations, most executives think of it as a nebulous, almost mystical entity. Most members of the leadership team will acknowledge that corporate culture is a powerful force. However, many think there is nothing that can be done to affect it. Culture can be understood and managed, but to do so is a difficult process that must be entered into soberly.

Implementing the Cultural Change

As stated previously, in an organization experiencing change, typically one-third of the participants will readily accept change, one-third will likely be concerned and look for clarification in the implications, while the final third of the organization will dig in their heels and fight change. The key is not to criticize or challenge the resistance because open resistance is critical to achieve success. The challenge is identifying covert resistance. Covert resistance results in all types of red flags. How to deal with this challenge is critically important in order to be successful.

The following leadership prerogatives and/or alternatives should be examined and considered:

- Redefine *organizational culture* to be more supportive of corporate business objectives.
- *Restructure* the organization to achieve a competitive advantage.
- Create p*erformance compensation* systems based on strategic priorities.
- Increase output capacity through the installation of *productivity improvement programs.*
- Establish *new products and markets.*
- Adjust to the *changing profile and needs of today's employees.*
- Increase the use of *computerized information systems and office automation technology.*
- Integrate new personnel through *expansions, mergers, or acquisitions.*
- Incorporate new *procedures* resulting from technological breakthroughs.
- Adapt to fluctuations in the economy by *downsizing.*
- Initiate major *reorganization* plans.

And, a methodology should be created for any one or a combination of the following:

- *Establishing the overall organizational parameters* within which to make change decisions.

- *Assessing the implementation risk* of major strategic actions before decisions are made.
- *Planning the implementation process* to minimize resistance and maximize support from those expected to change their skills, attitudes, or behavior.
- *Executing action plans* with a skill base that increases the likelihood of success.

The methodology when applied in an organizational setting will:

- Significantly increase the likelihood that a change will *achieve its goals on time and within budget.*
- Develop the implementation architecture that *generates high degrees of commitment and diminished resistance* from those affected by a change.
- Teach key people a *systematic procedure for implementing change.* The procedure can then be applied to specific projects on an isolated basis or it can be institutionalized throughout an organization and used to implement all directives requiring major organizational change.

Summary

Organizations seem to put all of their time, effort, and resources into identifying the need to create change and setting goals that will be achieved by change. However, hardly any effort or resources are applied to ensure successful execution. Change management is the issue and, therefore, a commitment to create a change management methodology is often the most efficient resolution. Therefore, the following examples are a few of the characteristics that successful organizations have displayed in the process of a culture change.

In effective organizations the process was:

- *Initiated and legitimized by top management.* Without sponsorship from the very top of the organization, no sustainable change will occur. Change initiatives without top-level, highly visible sponsorship will be perceived as just another meaningless announcement that will never have any real effect.

- *An integral part of achieving business goals.* Company managers must believe that the continued competitiveness and even the very survival of the company depends upon its ability to achieve long-range business objectives. The company's senior officers should ask: "What market are we trying to dominate?" The second question should be: "What kind of company do we need to be to achieve dominance in this market?" This contextual framework will help the company leaders define the beliefs, behaviors, and assumptions necessary for future success.

- *Measurable, with meaningful, tangible objectives.* Progress should not be measured by activity.

- *Implemented company-wide.* Everyone in the organization must understand their relationship to the ultimate goal of becoming a company driven by accountability.

- *The responsibility of line managers with support staff playing a supportive role.* Culture change cannot be sponsored by support staff, such as human resources, marketing or strategic planning personnel. Cultural change must be legitimized by leadership at every level of the organization with the authority and power to initiate and sustain the process.

Leadership of major change is not a simple process. There are no quick fixes when it comes to changing an organization's culture.

CHAPTER 12

And in Conclusion, the Beginning

> *"Remember, even a dead fish*
> *can get downstream."*
> —DR. ROBERT SCHULLER

This book has presented a prerequisite combination of fifteen significant principles and concepts that are much different from traditional methods of performance management. Following are the principles and concepts that must be adhered to.

1. Align performance compensation with long-term strategic objectives. Traditional incentive programs are short-sighted by nature. Management is typically rewarded to maximize annual profitability, while sales and customer contact people are rewarded to maximize annual growth (sales). The tactics to support these two objectives are diametrically opposed to each other. To maximize annual earnings a management team would not invest in people, systems, products and facilities to remain and continue to be competitive. Rather, they would drive everything to the bottom line. On the other hand, to support sales or growth, an organization must invest in people, systems, products and facilities to ensure that customer service and product enhancement allows the organization to remain competitive.

Therefore, traditional reward compensation methods are no longer valid in a highly competitive and global marketplace. The traditional corporate mindset is centered on short-term goals and its expression has been through rewards for short-term annual profit. As a result, there has been virtually no long-term strategic alignment of reward compensation with long-term strategic priorities.

What are the implications of this corporate mindset? An overwhelming dichotomy between short-term needs and long-term value with dire consequences for both shareholders and stakeholders as the future viability of the company is threatened—*if* people did what they are paid to do. First, if management has focused on short-term shareholder value (annual profit) they can do so only at the expense of long-term shareholder value. Second, the emphasis on short-term profitability, if carried out literally, would eclipse the priority of serving the marketplace, because an overriding emphasis on annual profitability will preclude management from investing in people, systems, products and services to create a more competitive company. The resulting inability to compete effectively would further erode both short-term and long-term shareholder value. That is why it is so obvious that successful management teams have never, ever, done what they are paid to do, and we can be very grateful for that.

2. Utilize a "balance scorecard" series of measurements. In order to maximize long-term shareholder value and ensure long-term viability of an organization, the organization must focus on the balance of profit, growth, quality and productivity. Multiple measures also create checks and balances and tensions between key performance indicators to ensure a business unit does not maximize one key performance indicator at the expense of another. Utilizing the balanced scorecard and multiple measures teaches all employees that decisions cannot be made in isolation.

3. Make sure everyone participates. The primary purpose of every business enterprise is to create competitive advantage in order to deserve and keep customers. The responsibility for customer acquisition and customer retention belongs to everyone in the organization. Therefore, significant reward for improved business results cannot be limited to a small group of customer contact people because everyone in the organization has a direct and significant impact on whether or not the organization achieves its fundamental reason for existing. That is why a contemporary compensation package includes significant reward opportunities for sales support as well as all direct sales personnel, and that concept must be coordinated and institutionalized throughout the entire organization. In today's highly competitive environment teams committed to excellence win every time. Limiting incentives to a few key individuals effectively benches the rest of the team and often creates an "it isn't my responsibility" syndrome. Allowing everyone to participate gives everyone a stake in the outcome and it also eliminates the tendency to entitlement.

4. Never put base pay at risk. The vast majority of the workforce cannot afford to allow their base salaries to be put at risk because it would jeopardize their standard of living. Many compensation experts recommend that placing base salaries at risk motivates employees to do better. On the contrary, it has been my experience that putting base salaries at risk creates resentment. Instead, base salaries and the incentive opportunities should become a part of overall compensation strategies. Recognizing this, incentive compensation can be used as a recruiting and retention competitive advantage.

5. Reward for results, not activities. Rewarding for activity leads to more activity. Instead, manage activities that create positive results and reward for results as they are achieved. It is important to create a comprehensive set of multiple measures that encompasses the income statement. This will introduce the entire workforce to the importance of business literacy.

6. Establish an equitable starting point. Baseline is a starting point from which performance compensation is created. Baseline is defined as a minimum level of acceptable performance that teaches everyone in the organization that there is a certain level of performance that must be achieved to justify base salaries and benefits. Secondly, baseline should be a level of performance that provides an adequate return to the owners/investors. Baseline can be driven from last year actual, a budgeted series of multiple measures, pretax income, return on equity, return on assets or return on investment. Incentive compensation should then be paid for levels of achievement beyond baseline.

7. Utilize "stretch" targets. In traditional organizations budget is the finish line. That puts a limitation on potential and the mindset to create high performance. Stretch targets encourage non-traditional thinking because they demand that people think in terms of market opportunities and how they can make things happen. Once the stretch targets are established, incremental, obtainable, increases of stretch between baseline and the target that maximizes potential should be established.

8. Weight key performance indicators mathematically. KPIs should not be weighted subjectively. Rather, they should be weighted mathematically based on the economic value created by the amount of stretch. Weightings then based on economic value will create a visible basis for establishing priorities. Employees will soon learn to focus on the measures with the highest weightings because it leads to the biggest incentive reward. In turn, they will have greater interest in learning how they can best impact those key performance indicators with the greatest weight. Arbitrary weighting provides nothing better than traditional subjective reward pool because it is not tied to actual performance and the creation of value. Equally important, subjective reward pools do not teach people how and where value is created.

9. Instill Consequences for unacceptable achievement. Traditional compensation programs reward people for achieving various levels of performance but rarely, if ever, include a consequence for not achieving minimum levels of performance. However, the lack of consequences or penalties is the single-most important reason why individuals and teams are often not motivated to achieve high performance.

An effective performance compensation methodology establishes a minimum level of performance for multiple goal achievement to rationalize or justify base salaries. A series of improved levels of performance is then specified, enabling one to create a matrix of multiple goal achievement. The matrix shows the participants' ability to increase their performance compensation based on the level of performance achieved for various goals.

An equally important facet is the creation of a matrix to relate penalties for achieving a level of performance below minimum standards. The weighting value for each KPI then reduces the incentive pool by the appropriate amount according to the value of each key performance indicator. By deducting from the incentive pool for results that do not adequately balance profitability and growth with quality and productivity, a significant influence is introduced for people to achieve above minimum standards of performance.

10. Establish self-funding reward pool. A reward pool can be self-funding only if the KPIs are mathematically weighted based on the relative contribution to value of each KPI compared to the total contribution of value in the stretch columns. Those parameters ensure a mathematical integrity for self-funding the incentive pool by sharing a portion of the precise and predetermined improvement of value. Due to the incremental nature of the model, there is no cap on the amount of incentive that can be paid. Similarly, there is no floor on the penalty for achieving levels of performance below baseline. This format allows employees to be able to see the incentive opportunity before the program begins, and to review the progress toward higher levels of achievement over a period of time. Converting the incentive pool to a percent of salaries then will simplify the communication of results.

11. Reward for subordinate levels of performance. Additional scorecards can be built to create a line of sight between day-to-day and overall organization performance. Additional scorecards will improve an organization's overall level of "business literacy," something that traditional profit sharing, 401k, ESOP and stock option plans fail to do. Any number and combination of scorecards can be developed for various business units at the regional level, divisional, branch/location, department, team and even for individual levels of performance.

12. Reconcile reward with performance. The sums of the economic value created by each scorecard must equal the value created in the corporate scorecard. When the sum of the parts equals the whole (reconciliation), we can accurately allocate the incentive pool; providing everyone with the same incentive opportunity as a percent of salaries. Most important, an acceptable level of profitability can be guaranteed no matter how much is paid out in

PERFORMANCE COMPENSATION FOR STAKEHOLDERS™

incentive compensation because reward will always reconcile with a level of performance. The highest performers will always receive the highest rewards, particularly if the Personal Development Assessment (PDA) is employed.

13. Initiate frequent feedback and coaching. Frequent feedback and coaching are prerequisite to the success of any program. The more frequent the feedback and coaching the higher the performance. Two quotes by unknown authors sum up this critical issue:

"I am able to influence only what I understand. What I do not understand influences me."

"If we don't change direction, we are liable to end up where we are headed."

14. Make it easy to administer. Data should be easily obtainable from your reporting systems and for the most part will be derived from the general ledger system. Although there is a learning period with any new program, the administration of the program should put minimal demands on personnel. In fact, an appropriately designed performance management system will reduce the time it takes for the budgeting process as well as all other critical processes such as financial planning, accounting and reporting.

15. Create additional deferred reward. The rationale for additional deferred reward for key managers and executives includes:

1. *Maintain focus on maximizing long-term shareholder value.* Deferred reward will reinforce management's focus on and commitment to long-term strategic objectives and management should be compensated in the future for decisions they are making today.

2. *Retain employees.* Deferred rewards create a "golden handcuff" to retain talented personnel who are committed to leading the organization to exceptional long-term performance.

3. *Reward for performance that cannot be measured within a 12-month time period.* There are many positions in various companies where the results of people's actions and decisions

today cannot be measured for several years. Good examples would be individuals who are responsible for lending in a commercial bank or for research and development in a manufacturing company. A portion of their reward pool should be deferred or an additional deferred reward pool should be created to reward these people for positive influence in their spheres. Overall, the deferred compensation costs next to nothing because creating additional significant rewards for a few individuals consumes a very small portion of the overall improvement in profitability.

Commitment

Ultimately, management's most important challenge will be to demonstrate its commitment to tie its greatest overhead expense (compensation) to long-term strategic goals rather than short-term tactical goals. Committing to high performance includes many of the elements of positive leadership: vision, enthusiastic belief, and accepting risk. It is commitment that will make or break the "*STAKEHOLDERS*" program.

Commitment is the underlying reason why successful people do what most people do not feel like doing, and they get it done. Every morning business life begins with choices. One can start the day *enthusiastically* or *unenthusiastically*. Every challenge can be an *opportunity* or an *obstacle*, and every disappointment a *learning experience* or a *failure*.

Commitment is what transforms a promise into a reality. It is the words that speak boldly of intentions. And the actions that speak louder than words. It is making time when there is none. Commitment is the stuff character is made of, the power to change the face of things. It is the daily triumph of integrity over skepticism.

Leadership

Early in this book, a reference was made to leadership as a matter of realizing uncommon achievement through common people. The University of Nebraska football team was given as an example where a program rarely has one of the top twenty recruiting classes but consistently ranks among the top ten teams in the nation. Their emphasis in recruiting has not been so much on acquiring the greatest athletes. Rather, the emphasis has been on the recruitment of basic skills and the capacity to understand the importance of work ethic as well as building team leadership. Coach Frank Solich took over the program in 1998 and has been associated with it since he was a 157-pound starting fullback in the mid-60s. He said, "The capacity for leadership has been the key factor in creating and maintaining a competitive team."

Leadership not only excels at the coaching level, but equally important, among the players on the field. "Often there is a lot of talk about leadership, but we have found a way of recruiting people who lead by their actions."

A challenging question for all members of senior management, then, as you seek replacement or additional employees, is: "Will your market allow you to recruit top-ten teams, or will you be capable of creating top-ten teams from the people you are able to recruit?"

Another challenging question to all members of senior management as you evaluate the key positions throughout your organization, including members of senior management, and all other managers and supervisors, is: "Have you selected people who do things right? Or have you selected people who not only do things right, but also demonstrate the unique characteristic of leadership, who focus on doing the right things right?"

For managers to have confidence that employees can make a much greater contribution by becoming involved, they must educate employees to understand how their company wins, how it keeps score and what it is they can do to contribute as individuals and as part of the team.

Knowledge Workers

One by-product of the information revolution is continuing education. As more and more knowledge workers work with their heads rather than their hands, education will have to be continuous. And that education will be delivered in new formats.

The traditional view was that there was little that could be done to raise workforce productivity, efficiency or understanding of business. Differences in output were thought to depend on whether the workforce was lazy or hard working, or whether they were weak or strong. But as the new workforce was studied, it became apparent that performance could be improved through improving business literacy.

Contemporary thinkers assume that people are ambitious and reliable and that a properly motivated work environment will result in each individual seeking to accomplish team and corporate goals. Contemporary thinkers realize that work can be considered as natural as play if the conditions are favorable. People do have the capacity and creativity for solving organizational problems; they can be self-directed and increase work performance significantly if the environment is created to foster self-motivation.

People do want to do a good job when they are doing it. Managers in organizations that understand this push responsibility downward, explaining to the workforce—the stakeholders—the reasons why things should be done while assuming that they have an interest in doing them and a willingness to do them. More important, they seek their input. They spend time discussing problems and asking for ideas and suggestions as to how the job can be done better.

The most important conclusion that can be drawn about this issue is that it is not an issue about workers, but about managers. Managers do what they do for or to workers because of what they believe about workers. Often managers are not as successful as they should be in the face-to-face process, primarily because of their own unfounded, erroneous and self-destructive belief about workers. In assessing your responsibilities as a manager, ask yourself if you would act differently if you really believed that all workers really wanted to be and were capable of being as successful as they possibly can be.

Scoreboard: Key to Untapped Potential

Too often management assumes people understand where their organization is going and how they can contribute to that journey.

The fact is that the great majority of stakeholders do not know what the game is or how we keep score, and many do not know how they contribute much less how their teammates contribute. How many people in your work environment do not understand how we win the game of business? Keep in mind that if the team members have no idea how the game is played and how to keep score, how can they possibly contribute to their full potential?

Alternatives to traditional management methods were bound to emerge. One new methodology is called business literacy, or open-book management. "*STAKEHOLDERS*" naturally increases business literacy through open-book management for all employee levels. That is necessary because the hierarchical models of management taught for most of the last century are no longer relevant and top-down management style precludes an organization from maximizing financial returns and providing the best customer service, let alone retaining the best employees. When "business as usual" predictability disappeared and as change and competition became dominant, the old assumption that management's job was to do the thinking and then transfer their thoughts to the front-line workers was bound to fail. Not for one, but for several reasons:

1. If customers were going to call whenever they wanted, answers to their questions had to be available from a range of informed professionals, not just from a few smart people in the know.

2. If a limited number of managers were the only ones with the big picture in mind, managing the needed changes to respond to competition and customer needs was going to be hopelessly slow.

3. If those employees incurring costs and making decisions impacting revenues could not read the income statement and the balance sheet and see their impact, then avoidable mistakes were waiting to happen.

Open-book management emerged as a set of systems to encourage all employees to operate at a higher level and to engage employees in the financial side of the business. As a prerequisite to success, "*STAKEHOLDERS*" asks everyone to be accountable for customer, financial and process results across the business.

If I Were a CEO Again: The Power of Written Goals

If I were a CEO again, my first order of business would be to ensure that every individual in the organization was taught the value of goals and how to orchestrate goal-setting for their professional lives as well as their spiritual, financial and personal well-being.

I would begin by reinforcing the definition of success: *Success is the achievement of predetermined goals that will create value.* Therefore: *People who do not have written goals, by definition, are incapable of being successful.*

Nationwide studies consistently relate that less than 3% of all the people in the United States live by predetermined, written goals. Yet those 3% have created 87% of the nation's wealth. That does not suggest that the creation of wealth is the most important goal, but it does underscore the importance of goals. People who commit and live by goals are successful because:

1. A decision is made and that decision plugs the hole where energy leaks.

2. Priorities are established so people are working not only on doing things right, but doing the right things right.

3. Vision becomes crystallized.

4. Challenging obstacles become opportunities.

5. Opportunities become achievements.

6. Achievements won't be given to chance.

7. Focus takes control of their future.

8. They are free to grow and free from pessimistic unplanned alternatives.

9. Enthusiasm is released by understanding where they are going and it fuels the effort.

10. Goals eliminate apathy.

11. Goals give hope and optimism.

12. Goals give excellence a chance to override mediocrity.

13. People become driven by accomplishment.

14. Priorities go from thoughts to marching orders.

15. Relationships are expanded.

16. Personal leadership is asserted because everyone knows what must be done.

And finally, remember, that a person without goals is like a dead fish, and even a dead fish can get downstream.

An Obligation to Maximize Potential

I recently had the opportunity to fulfill a lifelong goal to visit my family's point of origin in Ireland. The last family member to visit the homeplace was my grandfather in 1932. When I was very young I received a booklet authored by a distant relative. She assembled our family tree from the 18th century and told their story as "her attempt to dedicate the peripheral memory to our descendants who sacrificed so much so that we could have a free life."

My great grandfather was born during the first famine in 1846 and emigrated to America in 1871. His son, my grandfather, shared many stories including his childhood memory of awakening winter mornings with snow on his bed which had filtered through their sod house. In his adult life he was a schoolteacher, principal, farmer, rancher, started a lumber company that still operates today, and he was a state senator.

My grandparents had eight children. In their later years they continued to find many ways to be with as many children as possible. For example, every Saturday morning Grandma had pancakes for all the kids in our neighborhood, anytime 7:00 A.M. to noon. Kids by the wagonfull came and went all morning long. She was the first IHOP without ever knowing it.

After one traditional pancake Saturday my cousin John and I were asked by our grandfather to sit with him on the living room couch, a beautiful soft mohair, dark gray, more comfortable than any couch in the world as I remember. He sat between us so we could all read from a page in an 1871 Boston Globe newspaper classified section from the year his father came from Ireland through Boston en-route to Nebraska. Each classified advertisement on both sides of the page were for domestic help. Under each it read, "Negroes and Irish need not apply."

With strong arms pulling us very close, he leaned forward and said, "Always remember where you came from. Always remember how much our family sacrificed to create the life you have—a free life. Never ever think you are *better* than any other person. It is what you do with your life that will make your life *better.*"

That is a moment that has had more influence on my life than any other. Grandfather was teaching about freedom. Freedom was the prerequisite to realizing the power of human potential. I did not understand it all at the time, however I have been reminded of it often during the following decades and I hope my life's work has been faithful to his lesson.

Just a few years ago I was asked to present my performance management concepts at a national convention in Boston. The day before the speech I visited the John F. Kennedy library. Once inside the library, I walked through a timeline of events tracing the history of the Kennedys and the Fitzgeralds from Ireland to America. As I walked the descriptive panels I came upon the demonstration for 1871. And there, chosen by the Kennedy's as a focal point in Irish-American history, was a full page classified ad for domestic help from the Boston Globe with "Negroes and Irish need not apply."

On a knoll overlooking Galway Bay, the Higgins' point of departure from their homeland, I again thought deeply about where we came from, as the song reminds, "Where only the rivers run free." How difficult it was—the famine, the impositions by the British Crown—and how much they sacrificed to give us a life with freedoms we too often take for granted.

Realizing our human potential, then, is the issue. And with that the understanding that this wonderfully free life has but a single, most important, purpose. That purpose is to make a contribution to the best of our ability.

If we do in fact have an obligation to maximize our potential, and I believe we do, then inherent in the opportunity is our responsibility to help the people we work with to reach their full potential. We owe it to ourselves, we owe it to our families, we own it to our associates, but most of all we owe it to the people who sacrificed so much to give us the free life we now enjoy. It would be tragic if we did not expend every minute of every moment on this magnificent earth taking advantage of the unlimited opportunities that have been given to us.

My ancestors' story reinforces the well-known fact that human beings can only realize their potential when they are free to identify their talent and utilize that talent to the best of their ability. As I traveled throughout Ireland I realized it was the oppression imposed on the Irish people over the centuries that precluded their ability to perform and to understand their self-worth. Once the Irish people became free, they realized success beyond their wildest dreams. At the time I visited Ireland, theirs was the strongest economy in all of Europe.

Rothschild observes[1] that capitalism—the market economy, or the free enterprise system, whatever you choose to label it—was not planned. Capitalism just happens, and will spontaneously keep on happening. Capitalism flourishes whenever it is not suppressed because capitalism is a naturally occurring phenomenon. It is the way human society organizes itself for survival in a world of limited resources. He continues, "Just as a society naturally allows capitalism to flourish whenever it is not suppressed, because it is a natural occurring phenomenon…each and every individual is inherently a capitalist and will flourish whenever they are not suppressed." Therefore, it can be concluded that if every individual is inherently a capitalist, each and every capitalist will only seek other, less productive, ways when their freedoms are suppressed.

Applying that logic to the workplace suggests that the more freedom you provide your employees, the more productive they will be. *Performance Compensation for Stakeholders*™ is the catalyst to create a freedom where everyone thinks and works like an owner.

As we continue the transition from the industrial age to the information age, one of the great liabilities of history is that all too many people fail to remain awake to great periods of social and economic change. Every company has its protectors of the status quo. But today, our economic survival depends on our ability to adjust to new ideas and to remain vigilant in the face of change.

In closing, I would like to share the dedication I wrote in my book *Beyond Survival*, which was published by Dow Jones in 1989. It is applicable to those who try to protect the status quo.

An Old Irish Prayer

Let those that understand us, spread the word.

Let those who do not understand us, hear the word.

And for those who do not understand
after they hear the word,

May the Lord attend to them to turn their hearts.

And if He cannot turn their hearts, let Him turn their ankles,

So we will know them by their limping.

APPENDICES

Internal Service Quality Surveys

SERVICE QUALITY: OPERATIONS/DP DIVISION

There are 14 questions in the following survey. For each question, place the opinion value in the blank next to each question to correspond to your answer.

OPINION	VALUE
NO OPINION	0
STRONGLY DISAGREE	2
DISAGREE	4
AGREE SOMETIMES	6
AGREE	8
STRONGLY AGREE	10

Please consider each question carefully. Only select "0" when you truly have no opinion. "No Opinion" values will not be included in the average score tally.

_____ 1. I always get excellent cooperation from the Operations/DP staff.

_____ 2. The Operations/DP Division recognizes and responds to everyone in our company as if we were their customers.

_____ 3. In my opinion, our Operations/DP Division is customer-driven (researches our needs, then develops the systems and products) _rather than_ product-driven (designs products with little or no input from us).

_____ 4. The Operations/DP Division fosters a strong commitment to excellence, that is ... to being the best!

_____ 5. In my opinion, there is a general perception in our organization that our Operations/DP Division's services are unique in positive ways as compared to our competitors.

_____ 6. Our Operations/DP Division's structure is open and informal as opposed to bureaucratic and formal.

_____ 7. As change increasingly affects our industry, the focus on the Operations/DP Division is on positive opportunities, rather than on negative threats.

_____ 8. The Operations/DP Division has a mission statement which is fully understood and supported by everyone in their Division.

_____ 9. A strong and positive feeling of teamwork exists between the Operations/DP Division and other operating units of our company.

_____ 10. Mediocre or substandard performance is neither accepted nor tolerated in our Operations/DP Division.

_____ 11. When conflicts occur between our Operations/DP Division and other operating divisions in our company, a sincere effort is made by everyone to create a win/win resolution.

_____ 12. I truly believe that our Operations/DP Division is the best compared to our competitors.

_____ 13. *Measurable* performance standards in terms of quantity, quality, cost, and/or completion deadlines have been established for the tasks which comprise the responsibilities of the Operations/DP Division, and their performance is measured and evaluated as it relates to those standards.

_____ 14. The Operations/DP Division fosters a climate which encourages the top performers to stay and the worst performers to leave, rather than the other way around.

SERVICE QUALITY SURVEY: ACCOUNTING AND MIS

There are 11 questions in the following survey. For each question, place the opinion value in the blank next to each question to correspond to your answer.

OPINION	VALUE
NO OPINION	0
STRONGLY DISAGREE	2
DISAGREE	4
AGREE SOMETIMES	6
AGREE	8
STRONGLY AGREE	10

Please consider each question carefully. Only select "0" when you truly have no opinion. "No Opinion" values will not be included in the average score tally.

_____ 1. I always get excellent cooperation from the Accounting and MIS staff.

_____ 2. The Accounting and MIS Division recognizes and responds to everyone in our company as if we were their customers.

_____ 3. The Accounting and MIS Division fosters a strong commitment to accuracy and timely reporting, for example, credit application turnaround, expense reimbursements, order entry, shipping information errors, product reports, as well as many other reports.

_____ 4. Our Accounting and MIS structure is open and informal as opposed to bureaucratic and formal.

_____ 5. As change increasingly affects our industry, the focus on MIS is on positive opportunities, rather than on negative threats.

_____ 6. A strong and positive feeling of teamwork exists between the Accounting and MIS Division and other operating units of our company.

_____ 7. Mediocre or substandard performance is neither accepted nor tolerated in our Accounting and MIS Division.

_____ 8. When conflicts occur between our Accounting and MIS Division and other operating divisions in our company, a sincere effort is made by everyone to create a win/win resolution.

_____ 9. Overall, our Accounting and MIS Division find, generate and communicate a substantial number of practical operational savings ideas, and they provide exceptional internal controls (i.e., *"no surprise accounting"*).

_____ 10. *Measurable* performance standards in terms of quality and/or completion deadlines have been established for the tasks which comprise the responsibilities of the Accounting and MIS Division, and their performance is measured and evaluated as it relates to those standards.

_____ 11. I truly believe that our Accounting and MIS Division is the best compared to our competitors.

SERVICE QUALITY SURVEY: MARKETING

There are 13 questions in the following survey. For each question, place the opinion value in the blank next to each question to correspond to your answer.

OPINION	VALUE
NO OPINION	0
STRONGLY DISAGREE	2
DISAGREE	4
AGREE SOMETIMES	6
AGREE	8
STRONGLY AGREE	10

Please consider each question carefully. Only select "0" when you truly have no opinion. "No Opinion" values will not be included in the average score tally.

_____ 1. I always get excellent cooperation from the Marketing Department.

_____ 2. In my opinion, the Marketing Department is customer-driven *rather than* product-driven.

_____ 3. The Marketing Department fosters a strong commitment to excellence, that is ... to being the best!

_____ 4. In my opinion, there is a general perception that our Marketing Department's services are unique in positive ways as compared to our competitors.

_____ 5. As change increasingly affects our industry, the focus on the Marketing Department is on positive opportunities, rather than on defensive threats.

_____ 6. Compared to our competition, the Marketing Department's external advertising is significantly higher quality.

_____ 7. A strong and positive feeling of teamwork exists between the Marketing Department and other operating units of our company.

_____ 8. The Marketing Department's data sheet is formatted for maximum esthetics as well as clarity.

_____ 9. The *Newsletter* is esthetically attractive, informative and timely.

_____ 10. Overall, I think the quality of our brochures are superior to our competitors.

_____ 11. Overall, our trade show presence and presentation is superior to our competition and it provides a very acceptable image enhancement and Sales Return on Investment.

_____ 12. *Measurable* performance standards in terms of quantity, quality, cost, and/or completion deadlines have been established for the tasks which comprise the responsibilities of the Marketing Department, and their performance is measured and evaluated as it relates to those standards.

_____ 13. Overall, I truly believe that our Marketing Department is much more effective than our competitors.

SERVICE QUALITY SURVEY: CHIEF INFORMATION OFFICER

There are 10 questions in the following survey. For each question, place the opinion value in the blank next to each question to correspond to your answer.

OPINION	VALUE
NO OPINION	0
STRONGLY DISAGREE	2
DISAGREE	4
AGREE SOMETIMES	6
AGREE	8
STRONGLY AGREE	10

Please consider each question carefully. Only select "0" when you truly have no opinion. "No Opinion" values will not be included in the average score tally.

_____ 1. The CIO fosters a strong commitment to excellence.

_____ 2. The CIO fosters a strong commitment to accuracy.

_____ 3. The CIO reports are formatted for maximum clarity.

_____ 4. As change increasingly affects our industry, the CIOs focus is on positive, rather than negative, implications of those changes.

_____ 5. Overall, the CIO generates a substantial number of practical operational systems that provide exceptional reporting formats.

_____ 6. I always get excellent cooperation from the CIO.

_____ 7. The CIO recognizes and responds to everyone in our company as if we were their customers.

_____ 8. A strong and positive feeling of teamwork exists between the CIO and other operating units of our company.

_____ 9. When conflicts occur between the CIO and other operating units in our bank, the CIO makes a sincere effort to create a win-win resolution for all involved.

_____ 10. The CIO makes a significant contribution and sets a positive example as a member of the senior management team.

Personal Development Assessment

Name _____

Department_____ Job Title/Position _____

In Current Position Since_____ Employed Since _____

Date of Last Assessment_____

The Personal Development Assessment (PDA) is a vital tool to help our organization improve its overall level of performance. The contribution that each and every individual makes has a tremendous impact on how successful we are as a whole. As such, this PDA has been developed to help identify strengths and weaknesses. With this information, we can create an environment where individual strengths are recognized and utilized. At the same time, individual weaknesses can be turned into improvement opportunities. We understand that it is often difficult to talk about individual performance shortcomings, but we must be willing to address them. If we do not, we will never be able to make improvements in performance.

Instructions for Person Being Assessed.

1. It is important that you receive regular feedback regarding your performance. Therefore, a self-assessment must be initiated and completed every three (3) months. It is your responsibility to initiate the self-assessment.

2. Begin by rating yourself with respect to each performance characteristic.

3. Refer to the rating table on the next page for descriptions of ratings and any specific requirements that accompany each rating.

4. Once the self-assessment is complete, make a photocopy for your personal records.

5. Sign and date the submission box on the next page.

6. Submit the form to the person who conducts your assessments. The person who will evaluate your assessment should schedule a time within two (2) weeks of submission of this form to review it with you. If a time is not scheduled within the two (2) week period, contact the Director of Human Resources to let them know that you have submitted a self assessment, but have not had a review.

Instructions for Person Evaluating Self Assessment

7. Once a self-assessment has been submitted, it is your responsibility to review it and schedule a date to go over it with the person being assessed within two (2) weeks of the submission date.

8. Begin reviewing the self-assessment. Refer to the rating table on the next page for descriptions of ratings and any specific requirements that accompany each rating.

9. Any disagreement with a rating must be accompanied by specific remarks in the comment section of the performance characteristic.

10. Upon review of the assessment with the person being assessed, obtain signatures in the assessment review box on the next page. It is your responsibility to file a copy of this assessment.

11. If the assessed person disagrees with this assessment, they must document their reasons for disagreeing, and copies of all documentation must be submitted to the Director of Human Resources.

Rating Table

Rating	Description	Comments
5	Substantially Exceeds Expectations	Outstanding or exceptional level of performance. Far exceeds expectations with respect to performance characteristic. **Specific example(s) must be included in the comment section to support a rating of 5.**
4	Exceeds Expectations	Consistently performs at a level that exceeds the expectations with respect to the performance characteristic. **General comments to support a rating of 4 are required in the comment section.**
3	Meets Expectations	An expected level of performance. Definition of performance characteristic accurately describes behavior or performance of person being evaluated.
2	Needs Some Improvement	Generally meets expectations with respect to performance characteristic, but shows some inconsistency. **General comments that describe inconsistencies or shortcomings must accompany a rating of 2. A personal improvement action plan must be created with the appraiser for each score of 2.**
1	Needs Major Improvement	Regularly failing to meet expectations with respect to performance characteristic and needs help in this area. **Specific example (s) must be included in the comment section to support a score of 1. A personal improvement action plan must be created with the appraiser for each score of 1.**
0	No Basis for Assessment	No basis or personal experience from which to make a rating with respect to the performance characteristic.
N/A	Not Applicable	Performance characteristic does not apply to person being evaluated.

Self Assessment Submission

Date Assessment Submitted: _____

Signature: _____

Self Assessment Review

Date Review Completed: _____

Signature of Person Completing Assessment: _____

Signature of Person Being Assessed: _____

JOB PERFORMANCE

JOB PERFORMANCE IS IMPORTANT BECAUSE: Everyone in our organization must have the skills and ability to perform their job duties properly. As with any organization or team, we rely heavily on each other to get our jobs done. If we cannot count on each other to get the job done right, we will have a breakdown and will not satisfy the needs of our customers (the reason we all have jobs in the first place).

Performance Characteristic (Definition of "Meets Expectations")	Self	Appraiser	Comments (Use back of sheet as necessary)
Job Knowledge I understand what is expected of me when I come to work. I also understand what role my job plays in relation to the overall organization. when I don't understand, I ask others for help or clarification			
Job Skill I regularly complete all normal work tasks associated with my job. When confronted with difficult or unusual tasks, I can complete them myself or with some assistance from others.			
Quality I regularly meet quality expectations associated with my job. My work output regularly achieves desired or expected outcomes with error or problem rate that is acceptable for type of work performed.			
Work Speed Unless unusual circumstances arise, I complete all work assigned according to agreed upon standards of timeliness.			
Policy Compliance I demonstrate a good understanding of the policies and practices that regularly affect my job. I can be relied upon to comply with policy requirements without supervision.			

COMMUNICATION

COMMUNICATION IS IMPORTATION BECAUSE: It is the only way that we will be able to understand what is going on in our day-to-day operations, and more importantly, when special or unusual circumstances arise. If we communicate effectively as an organization, we will be able to work smarter, with less effort, and be able to satisfy the needs of our customers, suppliers and others within and outside of our organization.

Performance Characteristic (Definition of "Meets Expectations")	Self	Appraiser	Comments (Use back of sheet as necessary)
Responsiveness to Requests When someone makes a request of me or needs something from me, I respond in an appropriate, timely and complete manner. When required, I promptly share information with others in a clear and concise manner.			
Responsiveness to Feedback When I get feedback or suggestions from others, I do not become defensive, instead, I evaluate the feedback or suggestion and consider how I can change my behavior to better improve my performance.			
Written Communication When required, I communicate clearly and effectively in writing. Messages and/or directions are clearly understood by others.			
Oral Communication I communicate clearly and effectively. Messages and/or directions are clearly understood by others.			
External Communication I communicate with customers and/or suppliers in a friendly, courteous and respectful manner. I make a favorable impression during my interactions with others.			

INTERPERSONAL SKILLS

INTERPERSONAL SKILLS ARE IMPORTANT BECAUSE: We are a team, and a team that works well together has a tremendous advantage over teams that do not. Interpersonal skills are what you, as an individual, bring to the organization. Well developed interpersonal skills will not only benefit you personally, but will benefit the organization, and ultimately our customers. While it is important that our organization be made up of a group of people with a diverse set of experiences, backgrounds and perspectives, we all need a core set of skills and characteristics that will enable us to effectively function as a team and rely upon each other.

Performance Characteristic (Definition of "Meets Expectations")	Self	Appraiser	Comments (Use back of sheet as necessary)
Attitude and Cooperation I show a genuine interest in my job. I strive to create a positive organization climate. I have a good working relationship with the people that I interact with. I listen when others speak. I express appreciation and support for others.			
Team Player I place the "team" before personal interests. I accept my share of less desirable assignments. I give credit to others. I avoid playing "politics" and am not involved in unnecessary or trivial disputes with others.			
Integrity I demonstrate unwavering integrity in all my interactions. I strive to build mutual trust, loyalty and respect.			
Adaptability and Creativity I am willing to try new ideas and approaches. I am able to develop imaginative solutions and am innovative in various situations. I am flexible in dealing with different viewpoints and styles. I find a way to cope with uncertainty and ambiguity.			

(more)

PERFORMANCE COMPENSATION FOR STAKEHOLDERS™

Performance Characteristic (Definition of "Meets Expectations")	Self	Appraiser	Comments (Use back of sheet as necessary)
Judgment and Maturity I consult with others in dealing with difficult situations. I consider alternatives and consequences before making decisions. I recognize error or problems and work to correct them when identified. I am reliable and can be counted on to follow through on assignments.			
Initiative and Intensity I seek new challenges and responsibilities. I am a self-starter and finisher. I demonstrate energy, stamina, drive and enthusiasm. I am persistent in overcoming obstacles.			

PARTICIPATION

PARTICIPATION IS IMPORTANT BECAUSE: A successful team needs all of its "Players" participating. Not only on a day-to-day basis, but also in teams and meetings, for this is how we get feedback to improve performance and how we communicate changes that are going on around us.

Performance Characteristic (Definition of "Meets Expectations")	Self	Appraiser	Comments (Use back of sheet as necessary)
Meetings I have regular attendance at organization, department and team meetings. Any missed meetings are justified.			
Teams I willingly participate in teams or small groups and make a contribution to the team or small group.			
Training I complete required training assignments in a timely manner and I am able to demonstrate the new skills acquired during training.			
Attendance and Tardiness I show up for work and meetings at the designated starting time or within requirements. I do not exceed the normal absence requirements.			
Notification of Absence I promptly notify others of pending or scheduled absences or appointments. I provide documentation of such occurrences in a timely manner.			

STAKEHOLDERS

STAKEHOLDERS IS IMPORTANT BECAUSE: It provides focus and direction for everyone in our organization. In short, it is about what we do on a day-to-day basis and how we will be rewarded based upon how we perform.

Performance Characteristic (Definition of "Meets Expectations")	Self	Appraiser	Comments (Use back of sheet as necessary)
KPIs I have a working knowledge of all KPIs on the total organization model and any related subordinate models that I participate in. I clearly understand how I contribute to improving the performance of each KPI.			
Model Basics I have a basic working knowledge of the implications of STAKEHOLDERS model mechanics (e.g., weighting, scoring, calculation of reward, etc.). I understand how my performance directly influences my reward opportunity.			
Status Report Meetings I attend and make contributions during status report meetings.			
Action Plans I help create and participate in action plans to improve the overall performance of our organization.			
Personal Commitment I have created personal action plans to improve my overall performance on our team /dept. STAKEHOLDERS model.			

SUMMARY OF CHARACTERISTICS

THIS CATEGORY IS IMPORTANT BECAUSE: it provides a summary of critical categories not previously discussed.

Performance Characteristic	Self	Appraiser	Comments (Use back of sheet as necessary)
Function/Activity			
Accuracy			
Professionalism With Clients			
Office Management			
Teaching New Hires			
Office Appearance			

ADDITIONAL SELF-APPRAISAL COMMENTS

General Comments: _____

_____

_____

_____

My personal strengths include: _____

_____

_____

_____

The areas that I would like to improve upon include: _____

_____

_____

_____

ADDITIONAL APPRAISER COMMENTS

General Comments/Observations: _____

_____

_____

_____

Your personal strengths include: _____

_____

_____

_____

The areas that you need to improve upon or focus upon include: _

_____

_____

_____

PERSONAL ACTION PLAN

(To be completed jointly by person being appraised and appraiser)

My objective is to improve: _____

_____

_____

_____

_____

My plan of action for improvement is: _____

_____

_____

_____

_____

I will know that I have achieved my improvement objective when:

_____

_____

_____

_____

_____

My personal deadline for completing my improvement objective is:

_____

_____

_____

_____

_____

PERSONAL DEVELOPMENT ASSESSMENT SUMMARY

This form is to be completed by the appraiser, then shared with the person being appraised

Category	Number of Ratings in each Category					
Category (# of Characteristics)						
Job Performance (5)						
Communication (5)						
Interpersonal Skills (6)						
Participation (5)						
STAKEHOLDERS (5)						
Summary of Characteristics (7)						
Sum of Ratings (33) =						
	███					
X Weighting Factor	███	1	2	3	4	5
= Weighted Score	███					=

Enter Sum of Ratings here: ／_____

Personal Development Score: _____

Assessment Date	Personal Development Score	Multiplier	X Projected Reward Pool	= Projected Reward
Average*:				

*(Sum of Personal Development Scores/Number of Assessments)

Description	Score	Multiplier
Needs Major Improvement	1.00 - 1.99	0.00
Meets Expectations < 50% of Time	2.00 - 2.49	0.33
Meets Expectations 50 to 85% of Time	2.50 - 2.85	0.67
Generally Meets Expectations	2.86 - 3.14	1.00
Exceeds Expectations 15 to 50% of Time	3.15 - 3.50	1.05
Exceeds Expectations > 50% of Time	3.51 - 4.24	1.15
Substantially Exceeds Expectations	4.25 - 5.00	1.30

Instructions for each person being assessed relates that

- It is important that each stakeholder receive regular feedback regarding individual performance. Therefore, a self-assessment must be initiated and completed every three (3) months. It is each stakeholder's responsibility to initiate the self-assessment.
- Begin by rating yourself with respect to each performance characteristic.
- Refer to the rating table below for descriptions of ratings and any specific requirements that accompany each rating.

Rating	Description	Comments
SEE	Substantially exceeds Expectations	Outstanding or exceptional level of performance. Far exceeds expectations with respect to performance characteristic. **Specific example(s) must be included in the comment section to support a rating of SEE.**
EE	Exceeds Expectations	Consistently performs at a level that exceeds the expectations with respect to the performance characteristic. **General comments to support a rating of EE are required in the comment section.**
ME	Meets Expectations	An expected level of performance. Definition of performance characteristic accurately describes behavior or performance of person being evaluated.
NSI	Needs Some Improvement	Generally meets expectations with respect to performance characteristic, but show some inconsistency. **General Comments that describe inconsistencies or shortcomings must accompany a rating of NSI. A personal improvement action plan must be created with the appraiser for each score of NSI.**
NMI	Needs Major Improvement	Regularly failing to meet expectations with respect to performance characteristic and needs help in this area. **Specific example(s) must be included in the comment section to support a score of NMI. A personal improvement action plan must be created with the appraiser for each score of NMI.**
X	No Basis for Assessment	No basis or personal experience from which to make a rating with respect to the performance characteristic.
NA	Not Applicable	Performance characteristic does not apply to person being evaluated.

- Once the self-assessment is complete, make a photocopy for your personal records.
- The form is then submitted to the person who conducts each assessment. The person who will evaluate a stakeholder's assessment should schedule a time within two weeks of submission to review it. If a time is not scheduled within the two week period, contact the Director of Human Resources to let them know that you have submitted a self assessment, but have not had a review.

Instructions for Person Evaluating Self Assessment

- Once a self-assessment has been submitted, it is your responsibility to review it and schedule a date to go over it with the person being assessed within two weeks of the submission date.
- Begin by reviewing the self-assessment. Refer to the rating table for descriptions of ratings and any specific requirements that accompany each rating.
- Any disagreement with a rating must be accompanied by specific remarks in the comment section of the performance characteristic.
- Upon review of the assessment with the person being assessed, obtain signatures in the assessment review box on the next page. It is your responsibility to file a copy of this assessment.
- If the assessed person disagrees with this assessment, they must document their reasons for disagreeing, and copies of all documentation must be submitted to the Director of Human Resources.

Then, the procedure begins with the employee filling out a series of comprehensive questions about their development in the workplace.

The process reinforces empowerment, communications and most important a development of each and every employee in the organization.

Leadership: Self-Rating

Consider asking your managers and supervisors to complete the following survey. Ask each to rate themselves on a 1-5 rating, with 5 being a very good or high rating. Then, each senior manager should rate each participant and schedule a one on one session to discuss the differences, reinforce the strengths and resolve the weaknesses.

	Self	Manager
Each of your subordinates has agreed on responsibilities and standards of performance in order for you both to recognize achievement.		
You recognize the contribution of each member of the team and encourage other team members to do the same.		
In the event of success, you acknowledge it and build on it.		
In the event of setbacks, you identify what went well and give constructive guidance for improving future performance.		
You delegate, transfer decisions and accountability to groups and individuals.		
You demonstrate trust with those you work with. You provide adequate opportunities for training and (where necessary) retraining.		
You encourage each individual to develop their capacities to the fullest.		
The overall performance of each individual is regularly reviewed in face-to-face discussion.		

	Self	Manager
Financial rewards match contribution.		
You make sufficient time to talk and listen, so that you understand the unique and changing profile of needs and wants of each person.		
You encourage able people with the prospect of promotion within the organization, or, if that is impossible, counsel them to look elsewhere for the next position fitting their merit.		
At least quarterly you take time to personally assess the development of each person working for you.		

Creative Thinking Exercise

On a monthly basis, at a minimum, it is imperative that the workforce be led in a positive creative thinking exercise focused on "what do we need to do in order to maximize our potential?"

Creative Thinking Exercise: 10 Steps to Ensure Success

1. Identify the Key Performance Indicator.

2. Group into Tables of 6 -8 participants.

3. Ask each participant to make a list of ten to twenty (10-20) ideas the organization must do (action plan) to achieve columns 3 to 5 on the KPI. (Each person makes a list without discussing anything with the others at the table).

4. Have each Table Group appoint a scribe and a reporter/facilitator.

5. The Table Facilitator asks each participant at his/her table to identify one (1) action plan to improve the KPI. (The scribe makes a master list). Continue to go around the table until all ideas are presented.

6. The Table Facilitator asks the Table Group to prioritize top five (5) ideas or action plans.

7. The Room Facilitator asks each table to report one (1) action plan prerequisite to achieve columns 3 to 5 (and makes a list on an easel pad or board and continue to go around the room until all ideas are exhausted).

8. The Room Facilitator then facilitates the prioritization of the top ten (10) action plans.

9. Senior Management reviews the prioritized ideas, re-prioritizes them, establish preliminary deadlines.

10. Within two (2) weeks a person is assigned to each idea to develop a team to finalize the action plan, assign responsibilities for implementation with a deadline to complete each step in the action plan.

Work on a different KPI each month and when all KPI's have been covered, start over again. Discussions dealing with reasons why the company cannot improve beyond baseline are not allowed. Successful leadership does not focus on what is influencing negative results…rather, the questions need to deal with "what does your team need to do to achieve beyond the level of limitations you are now imposing on yourselves?"

First, facilitate the exercise among your senior management team to identify the most important key performance indicators. Ask the same question for each KPI: "What do we need to do in order to maximize our company or business unit's potential?" One rule and one rule only: "There is no such thing as a dumb idea. Think outside the box."

The exercise should be facilitated so that each senior manager can make a list of the things they feel they need to do and the entire workforce has to do to maximize each KPI. Initially, have every participant make a list without sharing it. Then, go around the room and have each senior manager identify one action plan that must be done to maximize the organizations potential. Write each idea on a flip chart. You should end up with 20 to 30 ideas for each KPI. Continue the exercise on each KPI until you have exhausted all the ideas from the senior management team. Then, identify the top five ideas for each KPI and commit to implementing those action plans by assigning someone responsible to be sure it is completed and establish a deadline for each action plan for each KPI. You need not orchestrate this activity in one sitting. In fact, it is probably more effective to take a couple of meetings to do this.

Over the next three to five months take your entire workforce through the same exercise, without lecturing, without telling them about your ideas, get their ideas on what needs to be done to maximize the potential of each KPI. Focus on one KPI each status report meeting.

If you have more than eight people in the room, break into groups of six to eight people per table. Again, have everyone make a list to themselves without sharing it with anyone else. Then, go around the room and ask each person to give just one idea that they have for each KPI, one at a time. Continue to go around the room until all ideas are exhausted. Again, make a list of the ideas that have to be worked on in order to achieve columns beyond "change of behavior" for each KPI, taking one KPI at a time. Then, have each table discuss and make a list of all the ideas that the table came up with and report to the entire room (group). Then, identify the top five or ten ideas, and create action plans, assign responsibilities and deadlines.

Within two weeks management must review all the prioritized ideas, identifies which action plans they can commit to and the organization goes forward with someone responsible and a completion deadline for each action plan. That's leadership and that is what *"STAKEHOLDERS"* is all about…defining what we can be if we are committed to maximize our potential.

Recommended Reading List

COACHING FOR PERFORMANCE: THE NEW EDITION OF THE PRACTI-CAL GUIDE by John Whitmore. Nicholas Brealay Publishing. London 1998.

STOP MANAGING AND START COACHING: HOW PERFORMANCE COACHING CAN ENHANCE COMMITMENT AND IMPROVE PRODUC-TIVITY by Jerry Gilley and Nathaniel Boughton. Chicago: Irvin

DEVELOPING HIGH PERFORMANCE PEOPLE: THE ART OF COACHING by Barbara Mink

LEADER AS COACH by David B. Peterson & Mary Dee Hicks. Minneapolis: Personnel Decisions Int'l, 1996

ACTION COACHING by David L. Dotlick and Peter C. Cairo. New York, New York Jossey Bass Publishers, 1999

LEADERSHIP YOUR WAY: PLAY THE HAND YOU'RE DEALT...AND WIN by Kim Krisco. Alexandria, VA: Miles River Press, 1995

MASTERFUL COACHING: EXTRAORDINARY RESULTS BY IMPACTING PEOPLE AND THE WAY THEY THINK AND WORK TOGETHER by Robert Hargrove. Pfeiffer and Company, 1995

"NEED A LIFE? GET A COACH." By Kendall Hamilton. Newsweek: February 5, 1996

THE CAREER COACH by Carol Kleiman. Dearborn Financial Publishing, Inc., 1994

"THE CEO AS COACH: AN INTERVIEW WITH ALLIED SIGNAL'S LAWRENCE A. BOSSIDY" by Noel M. Tichy & Ram Charan. Harvard Business Review: March-April 1995

THE CORPORATE COACH by James B. Miller. New York: Harper Business, 1994

"THE EXECUTIVE AS COACH" by James Waldroop & Timothy Butler. Harvard Business Review: November-December 1996

THE HEART OF COACHING, by Thomas G. Crane, 1998.

Preface

1. Peter Drucker, *Management Challenges for the 21st Centery*, Harper's Business, New York, NY 1999

Chapter 8

1. W. Joan Austin, Corporate Coach University International, Rochester, NY

2. John Whitmore, *Coaching for Performance: The New Edition of the Practical Guide*, Nicholas Brealay Publishing, London 1998

Chapter 11

1. Daryl R. Conner, *Managing Organizational Change, Dangers and Opportunities*, O.D. Resources, Inc., Atlanta, GA 1986

Chapter 12

1. Michael Rothschild, *Bionomics Economy As Ecosystem*, H. Hold and Co., publishers, New York, NY 1990

Michael T. Higgins

Mike Higgins was in industrial sales with the Aluminum Company of America, Director of a Regional Hospital Planning Council, EVP of a group of retail apparel stores and was president/CEO of a bank.

Those experiences provided a consistent theme ..."within every organization lies a significant untapped potential. Companies train people to do things as well as it can be done. However, they don't teach people where the organization is going, and how each and every employee contributes to that business journey. Most employees don't know how their company keeps score, so they never think or work like owners."

Higgins assists companies as well as nonprofit organizations in creating competitive advantage by achieving maximum performance for *strategic* priorities. He has assisted over 600 clients in the United States, western Europe and the Pacific Rim.

Higgins received an MBA from the University of Nebraska in 1976 and, subsequently, served on the Chancellor's Advisory Council. He has guest lectured on high performance leadership at the University of Nebraska College of Business Administration and the College of Dentistry, the University of Colorado, Nebraska Wesleyan University and Oslo Graduate Business College in Norway. He has been published extensively in trade publications and was contributing editor for a national trade association's monthly journal. He authored the ABA COMPETITCH on "Implementing a Sales Culture" and a book for Dow Jones, *BEYOND SURVIVAL, How Financial Institutions will Thrive*. He authored a chapter in

MARKETING MANAGERS, a management book co-authored by many PhDs and coordinated by two Northwestern University faculty members. Mike chaired the International Marketing Symposium in Norway where he also presented a paper on his performance management systems.

Michael M. Higgins

Mike officially joined MHA in 1997 after spending five years with the Deloitte Touche Consulting Group. During his first years with Deloitte, Mike focused on operations and business process improvement. The last two years he focused on information systems strategy and implementation. His project experiences include banking, insurance, manufacturing, utilities, non-profit, state government, retail, aerospace and defense industries.

Mike attended Nebraska Wesleyan University where he was an honors graduate in finance. He also attended the Graduate School of Business in Oslo, Norway, and then received his MBA at the University of Kansas.

During his college years, Mike played golf where he was a two-year All-American and a two-year Academic All-American. He was an assistant golf pro until 1991 when he began his graduate study in Europe. In 2000, he was the first golfer to be inducted into the University's Athletic Hall of Fame.

Give the Gift of
PERFORMANCE COMPENSATION
FOR STAKEHOLDERS™
to Your Friends and Colleagues

CHECK YOUR LEADING BOOKSTORE OR ORDER HERE

❑ **YES**, I want _____ copies of *Performance Compensation for Stakeholders*™ at $19.95 each, plus $4 shipping per book (Nebraska residents please add $1.40 sales tax per book). Canadian orders must be accompanied by a postal money order in U.S. funds. Allow 15 days for delivery.

My check or money order for $_____ is enclosed.

Please charge my: ❑ Visa ❑ MasterCard
❑ Discover ❑ American Express

Name _____

Organization _____

Address _____

City/State/Zip _____

Phone_____ E-mail _____

Card # _____

Exp. Date_____ Signature _____

Please make your check payable and return to:
DJI Publishing
1919 South 40th Street, Suite 213
Lincoln, NE 68506
Call your credit card order to: 402-489-0300
Fax: 402-489-0382